VARIETIES OF ENGLISH

Varieties of English

An introduction to the study of language

Dennis Freeborn
with
Peter French and David Langford

MACMILLAN
EDUCATION

First published 1986
Reprinted with corrections 1986, 1987, 1988

Published by
MACMILLAN EDUCATION LTD
Houndmills, Basingstoke, Hampshire RG21 2XS
and London
Companies and representatives
throughout the world

Printed in Hong Kong

British Library Cataloguing in Publication Data
Freeborn, Dennis
Varieties of English.—(Studies in English
language)
1. English language—Grammar—1950-
I. Title   II. Langford, David   III. French,
Peter   IV. Series
428   PE1112
ISBN 0-333-37996-9 (HC)
ISBN 0-333-37997-7 (pbk)
ISBN 0-333-40670-2 (cassette)

In case of difficulty in obtaining the cassette, please send
your order to: Globe Education, FREEPOST, Brunel Road,
Basingstoke, Hampshire, RG21 2BR. Please quote the title,
author and ISBN on all orders.

Contents

CONTENTS

Contents of the cassette tape

Symbols

Words or phrases quoted as linguistic examples are printed in *italics*.

A symbol in pointed brackets, e.g. ⟨d⟩, refers to its use as a letter in written English.

A symbol or word in slanting brackets, e.g. /u:/, /peg/, refers to sounds or pronunciation in spoken English, and uses the symbols of the International Phonetic Alphabet (see chapter 4).

In transcribing conversation, pauses are shown in round brackets, either in terms of their approximate length in seconds, e.g. (2.0), or as a momentary break, or micropause (.). When an overlap of speaking turns occurs, the place where the overlap begins is shown as //.

The symbol ∅ indicates a deleted element.

Note to teachers and lecturers: this book does not make use of the concept of the *phoneme* in discussing spoken English, although it is a fundamental part of the study of phonology in linguistics. Many students do not find the theory of the phoneme easy to grasp at first, and in the brief introductory survey of aspects of spoken English in chapters 4, 5, and 6, it was thought better to establish an uncomplicated approach to pronunciation, even though it avoids some basic problems.

This should not deter teachers from introducing the concept and using the term *phoneme* if they wish, especially if they are teaching the phonology of English as part of a wider syllabus in the study of the language.

Acknowledgements

The author and publishers wish to thank the following who have kindly given permission for the use of copyright material:

Sir John Colville for his letter to *The Times*.

Faber and Faber Limited for extract from 'The Waste Land' by T. S. Eliot in *Collected Poems 1909-1962* by T. S. Eliot; and extract from 'Cut Grass' by Philip Larkin in *High Windows* by Philip Larkin.

Mr Tom Leonard for his poem about the 6 o' clock News.

Oxford University Press for extracts from 'God's Grandeur' and 'The Wreck of the Deutschland' in *Selected Poems*, edited by Gardner.

Penguin Books Ltd for extract from Bede: *A History of the English Church and People*, trans. Leo Sherley-Price (Penguin Classics, Revised edition 1968). Copyright © Leo Sherley-Price 1955, 1968.

The Society of Authors as the literary representative of the Estate of A. E. Housman, and Jonathan Cape Ltd., publishers of A. E. Housman's *Collected Poems* for adaptation of 'On Wenlock Edge' by A. E. Housman text from OBEV.

Every effort has been made to trace all the copyright holders but if any have been inadvertently overlooked the publishers will be pleased to make the necessary arrangement at the first opportunity.

Introduction

The purpose of this book is to demonstrate how the formal study of language - linguistics - can be applied to written and spoken English in order to describe styles and varieties of language use precisely and accurately. The approach is **empirical**, that is, 'based or acting upon observation or experiment'.

Each text provides a distinctive sample of English in use. The descriptive commentaries show how a linguistic study can help to identify those features of a text which make it distinctive. The studies are not primarily concerned with evaluating the texts, to say whether they are good or bad of their kind, but will form a sound basis for critical discrimination where this is appropriate.

Chapter 1 looks at people's beliefs about, and attitudes to, good or correct English. Chapters 2, 3 and 4 discuss how English has changed in time over 1,000 years and more, and how it now varies according to geographical region and social class. Chapter 5 examines the differences between spoken and written English - that is, variations in the medium which we use to communicate with other people in the English language. Chapter 6 gives examples of the successive varieties of children's speech before they use, more or less, the English of their parents and other adults.

Finally, chapters 7, 8 and 9 present some familiar varieties of spoken and written English which are associated with specific functions, 'the language of . . .', styles of speech or writing which change to suit the occasion, the people addressed, and the topic under discussion. Studying the examples of style in English should help you to be much more aware of how you adopt an appropriate one.

In order to demonstrate this methodical approach to the description of style in sufficient detail, the number of topics has had to be restricted. There are many more varieties of English than those discussed in this book, but a similar process of analysis and description to that demonstrated here can be used on any other variety.

How to use the book

The chapters are subdivided into topics, and give exercises which should be discussed and worked before going on to examine the descriptive commentaries which follow. The commentaries are sometimes detailed, and are intended to teach important basic concepts about the language.

Some topics include further texts and exercises without commentary, but in the restricted space of a single textbook it is not possible to include many texts for additional study. Teachers and lecturers will be able to provide their own follow-up work.

It is not essential to follow the order of the chapters consecutively. Some teachers may prefer to select or to begin, for example, with chapter 5 on spoken and written English, rather than with chapter 1 on attitudes to good English.

The linguistic features which are described arise in an *ad hoc* way from the nature and style of each individual text. The book does not, therefore, cover all aspects of the sound and sentence patterns of English, since some may not appear in the selected texts. Others, on the other hand, occur more than once. When the linguistic features are identified, they are related to the meaning and function of the texts. It is hoped that teachers and lecturers will find the texts useful for other topics in English teaching which are either not mentioned in the commentaries, or only referred to in passing.

Teachers must decide for themselves how to relate this study of varieties of English to the necessary understanding of the phonology and grammar of the language which makes it possible. Theory and practice may be taught concurrently, with the teacher using the texts to demonstrate in greater detail those aspects of the sound or sentence structure that arise from them. Alternatively, the texts may be studied after an introduction to the phonology and grammar of English has begun.

In chapters 4 and 6 especially, students will need help from their teachers in learning to transcribe the sounds of speech and to distinguish the features of dialectal accent and children's language. The exercises provided are minimal, and limitations of space make it impossible to provide a more detailed, step-by-step approach to transcription. Chapter 4 is not in itself a complete introduction to the sound patterns of English, and presupposes additional teaching.

It is certain that only a limited understanding will be possible if the texts are studied without some model of language and its appropriate terminology being available to the student. The terminology used in this book is largely traditional and well established. Only those terms which are necessary for a satisfactory analysis or description are introduced. The accompanying cassette tape is essential for a proper study of the transcription of spoken English.

1

Variety, change, and the idea of correct English

1.1 Good English

You are reminded of the necessity for good English and orderly presentation in your answers.

This sentence appears on the front page of all the question papers of an A-level examining board. It presumes that you know what good English is, and that you could choose not to use it. The same word *good* is applied to spoken English also. The following description of a man wanted by the police appeared in a provincial newspaper:

He wore a tattered brown trilby, grey shabby trousers, crepe-soled shoes and a dark coloured anorak. He carried a walking stick and spoke with a good accent, the police say.

Exercise

(a) Discuss what you think the examining board means by 'good English'.
(b) The 'good accent' doesn't seem to fit with the rest of the description of the wanted man. Why is this? What would a reader of the newspaper understand by it, and how would he or she recognise it?

How useful is it to divide English into two kinds, good and bad? Our use of English varies according to a number of factors, and has to be appropriate to the occasion, the audience, and the topic. In speaking or writing English, we have to make choices from:

1

(i)   our **vocabulary**, or store of **words** (sometimes called **lexis**, so that we are said to make **lexical choices**);
(ii)   **grammar**, that is, the form that words take (word-structure or **morphology**), and how words are ordered into **sentences** (sometimes called **syntax**);
(iii) **pronunciation** in speech.

We have practically no choice in **spelling** in writing, because there is a conventional spelling recorded in dictionaries for every English word, without regard to variations in pronunciation.

The variety of English which people usually have in mind when they talk about good English is called **Standard English**, and is discussed in chapter 2. It has been accepted as the variety of written English against which other varieties are assessed. Some people speak Standard English as their normal dialect, and it is the variety you expect to hear on radio and television news, for example, and which you are expected to speak in school. You may hear people refer to Standard English when they are talking about a certain kind of pronunciation, but it is better to use the term **Received Pronunciation (RP)** for this, and to distinguish pronunciation from the vocabulary and grammar of dialects and varieties. (This is explained in chapter 4.)

1.2 A Letter to the Editor

The following text introduces you to a point of view towards English and its use which is typical of men and women who know what good English is. All newspapers publish letters to the editor, written by readers who have something they want to say and would like to see in print. Sometimes a letter will start off a series of other letters in reply, and public debate then takes place. The subject may be a serious contemporary political or social topic, or a not so serious comment on something that has caught the reader's fancy.

One subject has always been good for a lot of heated argument – the English language and how it is written or spoken. The letter to *The Times* which is printed below began a series in which twenty-one other letters in reply were printed, some supporting and some attacking the original by J. R. Colville (now Sir John Colville).

Exercise 1

Read the letter and make your own response to what it says, either agreeing or disagreeing. Examine the argument carefully. Do this before you go on to read the detailed commentary which follows.

The Times

LETTERS TO THE EDITOR

Correct English

From Mr J. R. Colville
Sir, I hope you will lead a crusade, before it is too
late, to stop what Professor Henry Higgins calls 'the cold
blooded murder of the English tongue'.
    It is not merely a question of pronunciation, which is
to some extent regional and which changes with every   5
generation, painful though it be to hear BBC speakers
describe things as formídable, compárable, laméntable, or
even, the other day, memorable. Contróversy and primárily
are particularly vile. However, the Professor's and my
main objection is to the mushroom growth of transatlantic   10
grammatical errors and, in particular, to the misuse of
transitive verbs.
    It would be a pleasure to meet you and, no doubt,
profitable to consult you on a number of matters. On the
other hand to meet with you, or to consult with you, would   15
be distasteful to us. The newspapers, including *The
Times*, are increasingly guilty of these enormities, and on
June 12 a formal motion in the House of Commons about
Maplin descended to the depth of demanding that there
should be a 'duty to consult *with* certain statutory   20
bodies'.
    Professor Higgins and I also deprecate the infiltration
of German constructions into our language. This is
doubtless due to too literal translation of German into
English by the early inhabitants of Illinois. 'Hopefully   25
it is going to be a fine day' translates back well into
German; but it is lámentable English.

Amongst the other adverbial aberrations threatening us,
the Professor and I, who were brought up to believe that
short words of Anglo-Saxon origin are (except when   30
obscene) preferable to long words of Latin origin,
strongly object to the substitution of 'presently' (which
used to mean 'soon') for 'now'.

All this, Sir, is but the tip of a large German-American
iceberg which, we fear, will presently become   35
uncontrollable.

I am, Sir, your obedient servant,

J. R. COLVILLE

Notes

Professor Henry Higgins is a character in Bernard Shaw's *Pygmalion*,
which was adapted as the musical *My Fair Lady*. He is a professor
of phonetics.

Maplin refers to a place which was the subject of an enquiry into
the siting of another airport for London.

Commentary

First, identify accurately what Sir John objects to in other people's
English usage.

(i)   Pronunciation

He finds the placing of **primary stress** on the second syllable of four-
syllable words painful – that is, he doesn't like to hear:

for**mid**able	com**par**able	la**ment**able
me**mor**able	con**trov**ersy	pri**mar**ily

You can infer that stress on the first syllable is his own choice, as he
later writes *lámentable*.

formidable	**com**parable	**lam**entable
memorable	**con**troversy	**pri**marily

Try saying them aloud and decide which patterns of stress you
usually use. Do different pronunciations cause confusion or loss of
meaning?

(ii)   'Transatlantic grammatical errors'
That is, features of English grammar which are thought to be typical
of American usage.

(a)   'the misuse of transitive verbs': **Verbs (V)** are **transitive** when they
are followed by a **direct object (DO)**:

           V   DO
It would be a pleasure to meet you.

           V   DO
It would be profitable to consult you

Sir John finds distasteful the form *meet with you* and *consult with you*.

Meet with and *consult with* are two examples only from a very large
number of **verb + particle** constructions which, especially in informal
spoken English, have been used for centuries, and which are still growing
in number. Many new forms do come from across the Atlantic, and the
term *Americanism* tends to be used against many other things and ideas
that originate over there, and which people dislike or distrust.

Such new combinations of common, ordinary verbs and adverbs
often supply new meanings. Try discussing with others what *to consult
with* means. Is it different from *to consult*? If so, is it a useful distinction
and therefore good English?

A look into the *Oxford English Dictionary* confirms that the form
meet with is recorded at least as early as 1275, and so has a good
pedigree. The verb *consult with* appeared by 1548.

(b)   'the infiltration of German constructions': Sir John's case is that
the German immigrants to the USA who settled in Illinois have introduced a German construction into English by translating word for word
from a German sentence beginning *Hoffentlich. . .,Hopefully. . .*

This use of *hopefully* is similar to our use of a large set of words
which are a type of **sentence adverbial** called **disjuncts**. They function
like compressed sentences, and express the speaker's attitude to what
he or she is saying:

Naturally I'll take you to the station.
Obviously she can't come.
Possibly he'll make it tomorrow.
Basically it's a matter of prejudice.
Inevitably they take a lot of persuading.

The use of *hopefully* to mean something like *I hope that.* . . may be
relatively recent, but it conforms to a well-established use of **adverbs**,
and it is difficult to understand what objection there can be to it.

The most amusing letter which was published in the series that
followed was from a correspondent in Germany, who questioned the
argument about the infiltration of German constructions into English
simply by writing a letter which was a literal word-for-word translation
of the German:

> Sir, It was me a small Bite surprising, the Letter of the
> Lord J. R. Colville, in your Edition of the 27. June this
> Year's to read, in which it says, that the english Speech
> to the 'Infiltration of german Constructions', owing to
> the 'too literal Translation' out of German onto English   5
> from 'the early Inhabitants of Illinois', succumbs.
>   Although it me unknown is, how these Persons of the
> Past spake, can i, as Resident the modern Germany's,
> thereto attest, that the english Speech most chiefly the
> littlest Resemblance with the Structure of the german   10
> Speech of the present has. Hopefully attests this Letter
> self that fact.
>   I might thereto also say, the Meaning of the Lord
> Colville, that there the Danger gives, socalled 'german
> Constructions' onto the English make 'the Tip of a   15
> german-american Iceberg, which . . . presently . . .
> uncontrollable' become will, a great Unsense is. Since
> when, so how my german Friends say would, is an Iceberg
> controllable? Perhaps means he that, the *Growth* the
> Iceberg's uncontrollable become would, if we not   20
> foresighted are. That can i also not believe, if i it to
> say dare.
> With the best Compliments,
> DAN VAN DER VAT
> Bonn

English and German are **cognate** languages, that is, they both originally developed from a common source, which linguists call West Germanic,
but their development over the past 1,000 years and more shows them
changing in different ways under different historical circumstances.

Is Sir John's argument from the use of *hopefully* sufficient to support his claim about the influence of German-American?

(c) 'other adverbial aberrations': Sir John states that the word *now* (a short word of Anglo-Saxon origin), is preferable to the recent substitution of *presently* (a longer word of Latin origin), which used to mean *soon.*

To refer to a dictionary to discover a present-day meaning of a word cannot be conclusive. Dictionaries are out of date as soon as they are printed, because language is in a constant state of change. You can, however, rely on dictionaries for past meanings, and for the origins of words.

The Concise Oxford Dictionary of 1976 gives the origin of *presently* as from *present + -ly,* and of *present* as from Middle English, which took it from Old French, a language directly descended from Latin. The Old English (Anglo-Saxon) word *nu,* meaning *now,* itself came originally from the Latin *nunc.* So to prefer *now* to *presently* on the grounds of its origins is not convincing if you take the word's source back far enough.

But is the meaning of *presently* for *now* a new sense? The *Oxford English Dictionary* tells us that it has had this meaning since the fifteenth century, and has retained it in dialects and in Scottish English continuously since that time. It came to mean *soon* in literary English from the seventeenth century. If its use to mean *now* has come from the USA, then it appears to be re-establishing its original meaning.

It is always something of a shock to hear words used in an unfamiliar way, but we should not assume that the speaker or writer is wrong, or even that the usage is new.

Exercise 2

Discuss the following letters published in *The Times* in response to Sir John's original:

(1)

Sir, I have much sympathy with Mr Colville in his
objection to the use of the expression 'meet with', which
is both clumsy and unnecessary, but it can hardly be
described as a modern usage, because it has the
respectable authority of Jane Austen, who uses it fairly often.   5

(2)

> Sir, It is a pity that Mr J.R. Colville in his excellent
> letter on correct English said of the infiltration of
> German constructions that it was 'doubtless due to too
> literal translation of German into English'. Nothing, it
> seems to me, was due or owed or required. Was it not   5
> *because of*?

(3)

> Sir, 'The captain advises that we shall be airborne
> momentarily' is a new piece of frightening illiteracy
> which now attends preparations for take-off. Hopefully
> the captain does not mean what he says.

Exercise 3

Write your own Letter to the Editor, either in reply to Sir John Colville's letter, or raising other matters concerning the use of English.

Exercise 4

Consult a dictionary and find out how the following words have changed meaning since they were first recorded in written English:

meat	deer	lord	lady	manufacture
sad	prove	starve	fowl	buxom

Here are quotations of older English sentences containing some of the words, taken from the *Oxford English Dictionary*:

(i)   Thy **mete** shall be mylke, honye, & wyne. (1440)
(ii)   Lamb iss soffte and stille **deor**. (c. 1200)
(iii) Settl'd in his face I see **Sad** resolution and secure. (1667, Milton)
(iv)   **Prove** all things: hold fast that which is good. (1611, Bible)
(v)   Here children **sterven** for cold. (1381)
(vi)   To defend them from Eagles and other ravening **Fowls**. (1607)

1.3   An Acceptability Test

1.3.1   Attitudes to English usage in the past

About a hundred years ago, a book was published for 'pupil teachers' called *A Manual of Our Mother Tongue*, written by H. Marmaduke Hewitt, MA, LLM. The subject called English was taught differently at that time, and it included the study of grammar, which was intended to teach the *correct* way to speak and write. This is called a **prescriptive grammar**. The English that was taught was Standard English, though it was not usually referred to by that name, because other forms of English were regarded as incorrect or corrupt variants of proper English.

A favourite way of trying to teach good English was to list the things that you should *not* write or say. *A Manual of Our Mother Tongue* contains a list called 'A Collection of Examples of Bad Grammar', and claims:

> The correction of errors is a useful exercise. It awakens and keeps alive the critical faculty, and serves to impress the rules of grammar more firmly upon the memory. All, or nearly all, the principal points in regard to which it is possible to go wrong are exemplified in this collection.

A modern reference grammar, like *A Grammar of Contemporary English* (1972), is a **descriptive grammar**, not a prescriptive grammar, and takes its examples from authentic speech and writing which was tape-recorded and collected in the 1960s.

A Manual of Our Mother Tongue is partly descriptive, but at the same time prescriptive in its claim to show its readers what Bad Grammar is like. It assumes that there is one correct form of the English language. A few of the examples of bad grammar are taken from literature, and include quotations from Dickens, Shakespeare, and Milton. Here are some of the 173 examples of bad grammar from the collection.

1.   Leave Nell and I to toil and work. (Dickens)
2.   How sweet the moonlight sleeps upon this bank! (Shakespeare)
3.   He would have spoke. (Milton)
4.   He parts his hair in the centre.
5.   Homer is remarkably concise, which renders him lively and agreeable.

6.   Who are you speaking of?
7.   This is quite different to that.
8.   What sort of a writer is he?
9.   I have business in London, and will not be back for a fortnight.
10.   'The boy stood on the burning deck,
      Whence all but he had fled.' (Hemans)

Exercise 1

Say what you think the correct version of these ten sentences was supposed to be.

The belief that we should all speak and write good English, but that many of us don't or can't, is still widespread. There is a lot of prejudice about forms of speech, which is related to social class distinctions as much as to regional variation.

The attitude of the late nineteenth century can be seen in this passage from *A Manual of Our Mother Tongue*:

> There are in Great Britain five principal dialects. . . . Distinct and separate errors of pronunciation are peculiar to each dialect, beside which one dialect often contains some of the peculiarities of another.

The author then asks the reader's pardon for 'the insertion of an anecdote'. He refers to a railway porter's pronunciation of 'Change here for Selby an' 'Ool', and says:

> It created some little amusement among the passengers from the South. One little man, looking around the carriage with a complacent smile and an air of benevolent superiority, explained to his fellow-travellers, "E means 'Ull'.

The implied superiority of the author and passengers from the South is clear. Everybody knew that it was wrong to drop your aitches, and that the pronunciation of *Hull* in the North was an amusing peculiarity of the natives, and not good English.

1.3.2   Attitudes to English usage today

It is an interesting project to test people's reactions to different forms of language, and to see whether Marmaduke Hewitt's prescriptive attitudes to usage are still held, and what they are.

The following sentences contain a miscellaneous collection of forms that are used, most of them being authentic, that is, they can be heard in present-day English. A few of them exemplify the 'bad grammar' that we are still told to avoid by some people.

Exercise 2

Test your own reaction to the sentences as honestly as you can, before going on to read the commentary. If you find one wrong, unacceptable, awkward or otherwise odd, try to say why, as precisely as you can. If you think a sentence to be normal or acceptable, don't try to find something wrong with it.

Remember that what you say, what you think you say, and what you think you ought to say, may be different. When you have thought about the sentences, or discussed them, you can try them out on others as a piece of linguistic field work (see Exercise 3).

ACCEPTABILITY TEST

1.   I aren't bothered.
     I ain't bothered.
     I amn't bothered, etc. (or any other spoken variant that is not *I'm not bothered*).
2.   I'm right, aren't I?
3.   We've got to finish the job by next week or we'll be getting a bad reputation.
4.   Jane met up with Bill in London.
5.   He failed to completely finish the examination but got good marks in spite of that.
6.   He's older than me, but I'm a good three inches taller.
7.   Don't you bother yourself. Let he and I do it - we can manage between us.
8.   That window's been broken for six weeks, but he won't do nothing about it.
9.   That's a funny looking gadget! What's it for?

10. He didn't turn up on time and I was sat there waiting for half an
    an hour. I felt a right fool.
11. Mary was elected chairperson of the Parish Council.
12. I can't see you while four o'clock this afternoon.
13. He omitted to lock his car door and found his radio and brief
    case were missing when he got back.
14. The two sisters are dead alike! You can't tell one from the other.
15. Hopefully it's going to be a fine day, so let's take a picnic and go
    to the park.

Commentary (an explanation of the language features which the test is
intended to question, with detailed analysis where appropriate)

1. One of the forms of the **contracted negative**, **present tense**, of the
verb *to be* is often taken as a **marker** of social class, and parents and
teachers may tell you not to use *I aren't/ain't/amn't*. They are dialectal
pronunciations, not used by Standard English speakers whose accent is
RP. An explanation is interesting:

(*a*)   The full present tense, negative, of the verb *to be* is:
     *I am not/ you are not/ she is not/ we are not/ they are
     not*
which is usually **reduced** in speech to either:
     I'm not/ you're not/ he's not/ we're not/ they're not
or to:
     I ? / you aren't/ it isn't/ we aren't/ they aren't
What form is used with *I* (**1st person singular** pronoun), when the word
not is reduced to *n't*? For RP and some other dialect speakers, there is a
blank – they use *I'm not* only.

   Why? Probably because *I aren't/ I ain't* is associated with 'vulgar'
speech. If you want to talk correctly, you don't speak like common
people. *I amn't* is commonly used in parts of Scotland, *I aren't* in parts
of the Midlands and North, and *I ain't* in the South. There are many
variant pronunciations.

(b)   There is a change in the pronunciation of the vowel in other verbs.
The reduced negative of *I cannot* is *I can't* /kɑnt/, and *I shall not*
becomes *I shan't* /ʃɑnt/. By a similar rule of sound change, *I am not*
becomes *I aren't* /ɑnt/. In each *verb + n't* the vowel /æ/ becomes /ɑ/.
But nobody regards *can't* and *shan't* as incorrect pronunciations.

(*c*)   A third observation on the use of *I aren't* is in sentence 2 following.

2. If *aren't I* in *I'm right, aren't I?* is generally acceptable, can there be any reason for not using *I aren't?* This form of **tag question** is completely acceptable, and it is often a shock for people who have just said that you mustn't use *I aren't* to realise that *aren't I?* is the same phrase in question form.

The explanation must be that it is a matter of social judgement, and the association of *I ain't* and *I aren't* with dialectal or lower class speech makes them unacceptable to some people.

3. Some say that you should avoid using the useful little words *get* or *have got to*, but everyone uses them, especially in informal speech and writing. It's a matter of style, not grammar.

4. Some don't like **phrasal verbs** like *meet up with*. Examples have been discussed in *A Letter to the Editor*. Try asking yourself and others whether *to meet up with* means (a) to meet by arrangement, or (b) to meet by chance. It is likely that you will get both answers, which suggests that the meaning hasn't yet been agreed and therefore that the combination is still new.

5. The **split infinitive**. *To finish* is regarded as a single lexical item, and is said to be split by *completely*. Ask where *completely* ought to go if the sentence is not liked. If you put it after *failed*, the meaning is changed. The split infinitive was an invention of prescriptive grammarians, and continues to be the subject of argument over style.

6. Should it be *than me* or *than I?* Some say that the phrase is a shortened form of *than I am*, so we should use *than I*. But *than*, part of the **comparative** construction *more/ -er . . . than*, functions very much like a **preposition**, and prepositions in Standard English are followed by the object form of pronouns:

	give it to me	she sat by him	we looked at them
not	give it to I	she sat by he	we looked at they

7. The problem is the **coordinated** phrase *he and I*, which seems to function differently from its separate parts *he, I*.

	Let him do it		Let he do it
	Let me do it	not	Let I do it

therefore *Let him and me do it*.

This is the grammatical explanation. Nevertheless, people say *Let he and I . . . .* Does it sound politer than *him and me* or *me and him*?

8. The **double** or **multiple negative**, very common in almost every English dialect except Standard English, is discussed in chapter 3.

9. In the eighteenth century, a prescriptive grammatical rule was invented for written English, that you should not end a sentence with a **preposition**, in this sentence, *for*. This is an example of a wholly artificial prescription, which attempts to counter a common feature of English with a rule based upon Latin usage. The dilemma for anyone who wishes to conform to this rule is shown in sentence 9. Is it English to say, 'For what is it?'

10. Some will object to *I was sat*, claiming that this is the **passive** form of the **active** *(Someone) sat me there*. It is, but not in this example, because the common sense interpretation is the same as the Standard English *I was sitting*. *I was sat*, and *I was stood* (also *I were sat/ stood*) are dialectal forms, certainly Northern, in which *sat* and *stood* may be analysed as **adjectives**.

11. *Chairperson, chairman* or *chairwoman*? The word *man* has traditionally been assigned two meanings: (a) a human being, or the human race, and (b) an adult human male. Meaning (a) includes male and female, and the argument for the retention of words like *chairman*, *postman, milkman*, is that the word functions like a **suffix, -man**, and is neutral in its assignment of gender.

The argument against is that the word/suffix -*man* inevitably implies *male*. The older word for someone who scrubbed floors and cleaned rooms was *charwoman*, because in English society men did not do that sort of work. Therefore there is no such word as *charman*.

12. This dialectal use of *while* to mean *until* is discussed in chapter 2.

13. Some people find *omitted to lock* unacceptable. The use of *omit* with an **infinitive complement** (*to lock*) is common in England, though not acceptable in the USA, where you can 'omit something', but not 'omit to do something'.

14. You will probably find objectors to *dead alike*. Grammatically, *dead* is here used as an **intensifier**, an **adverb** with the meaning *very/ completely/exactly*, but some would regard it as informal, even slangy. On the other hand, there are other phrases in which *dead* has this kind of meaning, and which are listed in dictionaries as Standard English:

dead stop/level/loss/calm/faint/silence/against/reckoning/shot/ahead

If these are acceptable, why not *dead alike*?

15. The use of *hopefully* as a **sentence abverb** or **disjunct** has been discussed in *A Letter to the Editor*.

Answers to Exercise 1

Here are the answers to the examples of 'bad grammar' from the Victorian grammar book *A Manual of Our Mother Tongue*, taken from the original under the heading 'Corrections of Bad Grammar'.

1. Leave Nell and *me* to toil and work.
2. How *sweetly* the moonlight sleeps upon this bank.
3. He would have spok*en*.
4. He parts his hair in the middle (*centre* means *point*).
5. Homer is remarkably concise, *a characteristic* which renders him lively and agreeable.
6. *Whom* are you speaking of? or, *Of whom* are you speaking?
7. This is quite different *from* that.
8. What *sort of writer* is he? - (not 'a writer').
9. I have business in London, and *shall* not be back for a fortnight.
10. 'The boy stood on the burning deck,
     Whence all *but him* had fled.'

Exercise 3

Find different informants - that is, people who will give you their own responses to the sentences in the *Acceptability Test* - and read the sentences to them. Ask them if there is anything that sounds wrong, and to explain as exactly as they can what is wrong. Tell them that this is not a test of their own use of English, and that if they find the sentences perfectly acceptable, they should say so.

Get your informants talking about good English, and what they think about the language. Ask them if they themselves speak correct English.

Find informants as different from each other as possible, in age, education, social background, occupation, both male and female, etc. See how differences in attitude relate to these contrasting factors. If you can record your conversations (with the permission of your informants), you will find it far more revealing and helpful to study the recording, rather than relying on your memory of the interviews.

Exercise 4

List other usages of English which are controversial. Try to describe their linguistic features in relation to Standard English. (It is useful to keep newspaper cuttings on this subject, and to write down in a note-book examples you hear.)

Exercise 5

Read the following extracts from a book published in 1864. They give us further evidence of confident prescriptive attitudes to the English language a century ago. The author was the Dean of Canterbury, Henry Alford DD.

Identify the features of speech or writing that he is talking about, the beliefs about language that underlie them, and say whether you agree or disagree with him.

THE QUEEN'S ENGLISH   Stray Notes on Speaking and Spelling
(a)   An American friend of ours, after spending two or
three days with us, ventured to tell us candidly that we
'all spoke with a strong English accent.'
(b)   There is an offensive vulgarism, most common in the   5
Midland counties, but found more or less everywhere:
giving what should be the sound of the *u* in certain words,
as if it were *oo*: calling 'Tuesday', *Toosday*; 'duty',
dooty. And this is not from incapacity to utter the
sound; but it arises from defective education, or from   10
gross carelessness.
(c)   Write good manly English.
(d)· The language, as known and read by thousands of
Englishmen and Englishwomen, is undergoing a sad and rapid
process of deterioration. Its fine manly Saxon is getting   15
diluted into long Latin words not carrying half the
meaning. This is mainly owing to the vitiated and
pretentious style which passes current in our newspapers.
(e)   *Desirability* is a terrible word. I found it the
other day, I think, in a leading article in the *Times*.   20
Reliable is hardly legitimate.

Exercise 6

Read this extract from a report on *The Teaching of English in England*, published in 1919. Is the distinction between 'English' and 'a dialect of English' a correct one?

> (a)   The great difficulty of teachers in Elementary
> Schools in many districts is that they have to fight
> against the powerful influence of evil habits of speech
> contracted in home and street. The teachers' struggle is
> thus not with ignorance but with a perverted power.   5
> (b)   The position of the English language in the world
> affords another argument for all English children being
> taught English as distinct from a dialect of English.

1.4   This is the Six O'clock News – belt up!

If you ask the question, 'Who speaks good English?', you will be almost certain to find that most people will say either 'the Queen', or 'BBC announcers'. It was the policy of the BBC from its earliest days in the 1920s to employ as announcers only those who spoke what was considered, by those with authority in the BBC, to be the best English – the accent that (it was said) everyone would understand – RP, **Received Pronunciation**.

In England RP is the **prestige accent** (though not in other English-speaking countries). If you speak it, you may be judged differently from another person who doesn't, either better or worse, depending upon who is listening. It is a fact that our judgement of what a speaker says is influenced by his or her accent.

An experiment was set up in which a lecturer who could speak both RP and a marked regional accent gave the same lecture, several times, to a series of different audiences who did not know the real purpose of the experiment. Lectures spoken in RP were judged by a majority of listeners to be superior *in content* to those spoken in the regional accent. How you speak, therefore (your accent), affects people's judgements of what you say (your meaning).

How might this affect our response to listening to the news on TV or radio? Does broadcast news in England have to be read in RP? If the news were to be read by an announcer with a broad Glaswegian accent, would it be taken seriously? Tom Leonard, a Glasgow poet, wrote a poem about reading the news. Listen to it on the cassette tape (Section 1).

Exercise

(Answer the questions before reading the commentary.)
(a)   Rewrite the poem in Standard English prose, and discuss what has happened to the poem in the process.
(b)   What is Tom Leonard really saying?

This is thi
six a clock
news thi
man said n
thi reason   5
a talk wia
BBC accent
iz coz yi
widny wahnt
mi ti talk   10
aboot thi
trooth wia
voice lik
wanna yoo
scruff. if   15
a toktaboot
thi trooth
wia voice
lik wanna yoo
scruff yi   20
widny thingk
it wuz troo.
jist wanna yoo
scruff tokn.
thirza right   25
way ti spell
ana right way
ti tok it. this
is me tokn yir

right way a   30
spellin. this
is ma trooth.
yooz doant no
thi trooth
yirsellz cawz   35
yi canny talk
right. this is
the six a clock
nyooz. belt up.

Commentary

The poem is spoken in a marked Glasgow accent by a newsreader. But newsreaders, even on Scottish regional programmes, don't sound like this, nor is the text what they might say. The poem makes us realise the attitude of superiority that Tom Leonard believes to belong to RP speakers. RP is one accent of many, but it is popularly judged to be better than others, to the extent that many people believe that RP is English spoken without an accent.

By inverting the relationship between present-day RP (a Southern English educated accent) and working-class Glaswegian Scottish, Tom Leonard jolts us into examining snobbish attitudes towards a Scottish urban accent. The poem could only have been the voice of a BBC newsreader if the past history of Scotland and England had been different, and if Glasgow were the capital of Great Britain. The Glasgow dialect would then have been Standard English, and RP would have been educated Glasgow Scots, because the centre of political and economic influence would have been in Glasgow, not London.

Prestige dialects and accents do not arise because of their beauty or linguistic superiority, but because those who originally speak them are influential, and others copy them.

During the 1939–45 war, the Yorkshire broadcaster Wilfred Pickles was employed to read the news in his Halifax accent, but the attempt to use his popularity as an entertainer to make the news more homely completely failed. (Listen to Section 2 of the cassette tape.) There were many complaints. People 'couldn't believe the news' if it was read in a regional dialectal accent. 'If a toktaboot thi trooth lik wanna yoo scruff yi widny thingk it wuz troo.'

If, in addition, 'yooz doan no thi trooth yirseltz cawz yi canny talk right', it makes the possession of a prestige accent essential for *understanding the truth*, as well as for getting on in the world. Is this an argument to be taken seriously?

(The historical development of Standard English is discussed in chapter 2, and dialectal accent and attitudes to pronunciation in chapter 4.)

1.5   Is there a language trap?

The debate about the use of Standard English and the status of dialectal English continues to arouse controversy.

Exercise

(a)   Read, discuss and evaluate the following extracts: (1) is from *Accent, Dialect and the School* by Professor Peter Trudgill, published in 1975, and (2) is from *The Language Trap: Race, Class and the 'Standard English' issue in British Schools*, by Professor John Honey, published in 1983.

(b)   Discuss the practical consequences of using dialectal and non-standard English in situations where Standard English is expected.

(1)   There are no linguistic reasons for saying that any language is superior to any other. All languages, that is, are equally 'good'. There is no way of evaluating any language more favourably than any other. Linguists have found that all languages are complex systems which are   5
equally valid as means of communication . . . .. They are also no different in their expressive capabilities . . . .

The fact that no one language is 'better' than any other is important for the role of language in education. This is because the same thing is equally true of different   10
varieties of the same language. Just as there is no reason for arguing that Gaelic is superior to Chinese, so no English dialect can be claimed to be linguistically superior or inferior to any other. All English dialects are equally complex, structured and valid linguistic   15
systems.

(2)   It is a serious matter that our educational system
(and others) continue to turn out, as they do, an annual
crop of total illiterates, and no less serious that from
otherwise able pupils we produce students who are in some
sense semi-literate. Yet the inability of our schools to   5
turn out pupils with satisfactory standards of English is
not simply due to the legacy of an inappropriate English
curriculum or to a shortage of appropriately qualified
teachers. Another powerful factor has been at work,
especially over the past decade, and its effect has been   10
to undermine attempts by teachers to meet the demands of
parents and employers that pupils should be able to speak
and write 'good English'. This is the notion, propounded
originally by a group of specialists in linguistics, and
widely influential among educationists and especially   15
among teachers of English and those who train them, that
for schools to foster one variety of English is contrary
to the findings of the science of linguistics. For has
that newly established discipline not demonstrated that
all languages, and all varieties of any one language, are   20
equally good? Therefore, to emphasise any one variety,
i.e. standard English, in preference to the dialect spoken
in the pupil's home, is not only unjustifiable in
scientific terms, but it does irreparable harm to the
self-esteem of the child whose dialect is discriminated   25
against.

2

Dialects and Standard English – the past

2.1 How the English language was brought to Britain

The English language was brought to the island Britannia in the first half of the fifth century AD by settlers called Angles from across the North Sea. Britannia was the Latin name for the island, which had been a colony of the Roman Empire since the conquest which began in AD 43. The inhabitants are referred to as Britons or Celts. When the Roman legions were withdrawn from Britannia early in the fifth century to help in the defence of the empire, the Britons were left to defend themselves against attacks from the west and north (present-day Ireland and Scotland). The Angles were at first invited from across the North Sea to assist the Britons in defending the country, and were granted lands in the eastern part of the island:

> nevertheless, their real intention was to attack it. At
> first they engaged the enemy advancing from the north, and
> having defeated them, sent back news of their success to
> their homeland, adding that the country was fertile and
> the Britons cowardly. Whereupon a larger fleet quickly   5
> came over with a great body of warriors, which, when
> joined to the original forces, constituted an invincible
> army. These new-comers were from the three most
> formidable races of Germany, the Saxons, Angles, and
> Jutes. (From Bede's *History of the English Church and*   10
> *People*, translated by Leo Sherley-Price)

The invaders spoke dialects of a language family which scholars now call **West Germanic**; the Britons spoke dialects of **Celtic**. In time, the country became known as *Englalond* - Angle-land - and the language as *Englisc*. We now call the language of this early period, up to about

22

1100 or 1150, **Old English**. The Britons were called *Wealas* in Old English, which is the same as the modern English word *Welsh*. Many of them were driven westwards, to settle in Wales and Cornwall. Later on, there were migrations of Britons into France, to the northern parts known as Bretagne (or Brittany) and Normandy. Today Celtic languages are still spoken (for example Welsh, Scots Gaelic, Irish Gaelic and Breton), though there are hardly any words of Celtic in the English language.

Although we speak of Old English as a **language**, there was no single standard version of it. There were four distinct dialects:

1. Northumbrian – spoken north of the river Humber;
2. Mercian – in the Midlands from East Anglia across westwards to the Welsh border;
3. Kentish – in the south-east;
4. West Saxon – in the south and south-west.

They are called **dialects** because they were mutually intelligible varieties of the same language. That is, you could talk with a speaker of another dialect and be understood, though mutual understanding could be difficult. There is evidence of this difficulty as late as the fourteenth century, when John of Trevisa wrote, in the South-Western dialect of **Middle English**:

Al the longage of the Norþumbres, and specialych at York, ys so scharp, slyttyng and frotyng, and unschape, þat we Souþeron men may þat longage unneþe undurstonde.

(All the speech of the Northumbrians, and especially at York, is so sharp, piercing and grinding, and unformed, that we Southerners can hardly understand it.)

The evidence for the different dialects comes from the surviving manuscripts of the period. When the same words are regularly spelt differently, we can assume that they are pronounced differently, because Old English was spelt more or less as it sounded.

The establishment of a **standard language** depends upon the kind of social and political organisation in a country which did not develop in England until the sixteenth century.

2.2 Britain before the English came

We rely for much of our knowledge of the early history of England on *The History of the English Church and People*, written in Latin by Bede and completed in 731 in the monastery of Jarrow, in Northumberland. To introduce you to some of the important historical events which were to affect the development of the Old English language, here are two extracts from Bede's *History*. The book was translated from the Latin at different periods, so we can also illustrate, at the same time, changes in the language itself, by using four translations: (a) twentieth, (b) sixteenth, (c) fourteenth and (d) ninth century.

(1) A description of 'Britannia', the Roman colony

(a) In old times, the country had twenty-eight noble cities and innumerable castles, all of which were guarded by walls, towers, and barred gates.

(b) This Iland had in it sumtimes xxviii cities, beside an innumerable sort of castles whiche also wer well and strongly fensyd wyth walles, turrettes, gates, and bullwarkes.   5

(c) The kyngdom of Bretayne was somtymes i-hight wiþ eiȝte and twenty noble citees, wiþoute welle many castelles þat were wiþ walles, wiþ toures, wiþ ȝates, wiþ barres, stalworþliche i-buld.   10

(d) Wæs dis ealond geo gewurþad mid þam æþelestrum
was this island once made splendid with the noblest
ceastrum, twega wana þrittigum, þa þe wæron mid
cities   two less than thirty those that were with
weallum and torrum and geatum and þam trumestum locum
walls   and towers and gates   and the firmest   bars
getimbrade, butan oþrum læssan unrim   ceastra.   15
built   besides other   lesser   innumerable towns.

(2) The first inhabitants of Britain

(a) The original inhabitants of the island were the Britons, from whom it takes its name, and who, according

to tradition, crossed into Britain from Armorica, and
occupied the southern parts.

(b) At the first this land was inhabited of none other   5
nation but only of the Brittanes, of whom it receiveth his
name: which Britannes comyng out of Armorica (called now
little Britany) as it is thought, chose unto them selves
the sowth parte of this land.

(c) Bretouns wonede first in þis ilond. þei come hider   10
and took hir cours from Armorik, þat now is þe oþer
Bretayne; þey helde long tyme þe souþ contrayes of þe
ilond.

(d) On fruman ærest wæron þysses ealondes bigengan
in beginning first were of this island's inhabitants
Bryttes ane, fram þam hit naman onfeng. Is þæt sæd,   15
Britons once from them it name received is it   said
þæt hi comon fram Armoricano þære mægeþe on Breotone,
that they came from Armorica the   people   in Britanny
and þa suþdælas þysses ealondes him gesæton and
and the southern parts of this island's them settled and
geahnodon.
possessed.

Commentary

The Old English extracts are in the West Saxon dialect. You will notice
several words which are still in modern English, though their spelling,
and often their pronunciation also, has changed:

ealond (island)	timbr- (timber = to build)
þrittig (thirty)	oþer (other)
wær- (were)	læs (less)
weall (wall)	ceaster (-caster, -chester)
torr (tower)	nama (name)
geat (gate)	suþ (south)
loc (lock, bar)	sett- (to set down)
s æd (said)	fram (from)

Exercise

Compare the list with the way the words are spelt in the texts, and
write them out with their endings, or **suffixes**, which have been omitted
in the list. You should find the following: *-um*, *-on*, *-an*, *-de*, *-es*, *-as*,
-a, *-e*.

These suffixes are essential in the grammar of Old English, and one of
the most important changes in the language has been the gradual loss of
almost all of them. Suffixes are also called **inflections**. Old English was
a highly **inflected** language. Notice also the words translated by *the*:
þam, þ re; there are eight other forms for *the*.

   Old English was written down using the Roman alphabet, but other
useful letters were adopted to represent English sounds that did not
occur in the pronunciation of Latin. Two of these letters, reproduced
above, are ⟨þ⟩ (thorn), for which we now use ⟨th⟩, and ⟨æ⟩ (ash), for
which we now have to use ⟨a⟩, and so can no longer distinguish in
spelling between the vowels of *ash* and *father*, /æ/ and /ɑ/. Other Old
English letters, not usually reproduced in modern printed versions, were
⟨ƿ⟩ (wynn) for ⟨w⟩, ⟨ȝ⟩ (yogh) for ⟨g⟩, and ⟨ð⟩ (eth), an alternative letter
for ⟨þ⟩. Middle English writing introduced ⟨g⟩ and kept ⟨ȝ⟩, to distinguish
between two different sounds.

   Other Old English words in the two extracts above have been lost.
The reason for this will be clearer when you examine two later historical
events which had profound effects on the language.

2.3 The Vikings

The Angles, Saxons and Jutes, over a period of two hundred years, had
gradually occupied almost the whole of England, but after about three
hundred years of settlement, with the country divided into seven
kingdoms, Vikings from Scandinavia began a series of raids on the North
and East of England, at first for plunder, and then for occupation and
settlement. The events were recorded in the contemporary *Anglo-Saxon
Chronicle*.

   In the following extracts, the inflections are printed in bold type.

   AD 787 Her com**on** ærest III scip**u** Norþmanna of
      Here came first   3 ships of Northmen from

Hereþelande, and þa se gerefa þær to rad, and hi
Herethaland   and then the reeve there to rode and them
wolde drifan to þes cyninges tune, þy he nyste
wished to drive to the king's town because he knew not
hwæt hi wæron, and hine man ofsloh þa. þa wæron þa
what they were   and him   one slew then. Those were the
erestan scipu Deniscra manna þe Angelcynnes land   5
first   ships of Danish men that English people's land
gesohton.
sought.

After a hundred years of intermittent warfare, the king of Wessex,
Alfred, finally defeated the Vikings, but had to allow them to occupy
the northern and eastern parts of England, which were known as the
Danelaw.

AD 878 Her Ælfred cyning gefeaht wiþ ealne
        Here Alfred king   fought against all
here, and hine geflymde, and him æfter rad oþ þæt
(the) enemy & him put to flight, & him after rode to the
geweorc, and þær sæt xiiii niht, and þa sealde se here
fort   and there sat 14   nights and then gave the enemy
him gislas and myccle aþas, þæt hi of his rice
him hostages & great oaths that they from his kingdom
woldon, and him eac geheton þæt heora cyning fulwihte   5
would (go) & him also promised that their king baptism
onfon wolde, and hi þæt gelaston.
receive would & they that performed.

Exercise

Compare the Old English texts with the word-for-word translation
underneath. What differences in word-order are there between Old and
present-day English?

You can still hear something of the effects of the Viking settlement by
listening to present-day northern dialects of English. The Vikings spoke
dialects of a Scandinavian language, now called **Old Norse**, which was
sufficiently similar to Old English that speakers of the two languages

could communicate with each other. Both languages were Germanic. Many of their words were similar. But the grammatical inflections were different, so that where Vikings and English lived near each other and had regular speech together, the suffixes tended to be left off.

This speeded up the loss of word-endings, which was taking place anyway in Old English because the inflections were unstressed syllables. But the Vikings also had words in Old Norse which did not have their Old English cognate equivalents, and many of these remained in Northern dialects. Some have in fact replaced Old English words, and have spread throughout Standard English and the other Southern dialects, for example:

they	sister	skin
them	call	sky
their	egg	skirt (cp shirt)
kneel	leg	take

These words were all Old Norse. So the source of English dialects today, including Standard English, lies partly in the four dialects of Old English, and also in the blend of Old Norse dialects spoken by the Viking settlers in the Danelaw, which eventually merged with English.

2.4 The Norman Conquest

The second historical event of the greatest importance is probably known to everyone through the date - 1066. This was the conquest of England by William, Duke of Normandy. The Normans (Northmen) came of Viking stock also, but after settling in northern France they had adopted the French language. The dialect they spoke is known as Old Northern French.

AD 1066 And þa hwile com Willelm eorl upp æt
           and meanwhile came William earl up at
Hestingan, on Sancte Michaeles mæssedæg, and Harold com
Hastings   on Saint   Michael's mass-day   and Harold came
norþan, and him wiþ gefeaht ear þan þe his here come eall,
from the north & him with fought before his army came all
and þær he feoll, and Willelm þis land geeode and com
and there he fell and William this land occupied & came

to Westmynstre, and Ealdred arcebiscop hine to cynge   5
to Westminster   and Ealdred archbishop him as king
gehalgode.
consecrated.

The effect on the English language was not to be fully felt for two
hundred years or more, but by the end of the fourteenth century, in
the time of the poet Chaucer, hundreds of words of French origin had
been taken into English. Here is a short extract from Chaucer's *Canterbury Tales*. The words of French origin have been printed in italics.

In *Flaundres* whilom was a *compaignye*
Of yonge folk that *haunteden folye*,
As *riot*, *hasard*, *stywes*, and *tavernes*,
Where as with harpes, *lutes*, *and gyternes*,
They *daunce* and *pleyen* at *dees* bothe day and nyght,   5
And eten also and drynken over hir myght,
Thurgh which they doon the devel *sacrifise*
Withinne that develes temple, in cursed wise,
By *superfluytee abhomynable*.

After 1066, authority in government, land-ownership and the
Church was almost completely given to French-speaking Normans. The
writing of Old English was much reduced, and when we look at the
language from about 1150 to 1450, **Middle English**, we find marked
differences from Old English in spelling, as well as changes in vocabulary,
word-forms and grammar.

Once a spelling system is adopted and becomes standardised, writers
ignore those changes in pronunciation that always develop, firstly
between different dialect speakers, and secondly between one generation
of speakers and another. This had begun to happen before the Norman
conquest. In the tenth and eleventh centuries, West Saxon was becoming
the standard written language. West Saxon spelling was used in writing
in the other dialect areas of England, and changes in the pronunciation
of West Saxon itself were not systematically recorded in the spelling.
This process was interrupted as a result of the Norman conquest. The
Old English tradition was lost, and French-speaking scribes, when
writing English, tended to write what they heard. As a result, we have
plenty of evidence of the differences between Middle English dialects.

Today we have a spelling system which has remained almost un-
changed since the middle of the eighteenth century, and which even
then represented the pronunciation of English at the end of the fourteenth century. This helps to explain why English spelling seems so
remote from its pronunciation. Pronunciation has changed a lot in 600
years, but the spelling has not kept up with it.

Exercise

Look up the modern equivalents of the words of the Caxton text in
the following section 2.5, using a distionary that gives the **etymology**,
or historical source of words.

Make a list of those that came from Old English, Old Norse, or
French. What is the proportion from each source? Do any particular
kinds of word belong to one source?

2.5 The establishment of Standard English

As the short extracts from Bede's *History* showed, the changes that
have taken place in the English language can be demonstrated by
examining texts written down at different times. Here for example is
the same text in versions only one hundred years apart. It is from John
of Trevisa's account of the English language, firstly in his own English
of about 1385, and then in a modernised version printed by William
Caxton in 1482. The fourteenth-century text has present-day punctuation; Caxton's has the original punctuation.

Exercise

(a)   Examine the two texts in detail, and list the changes from four-
      teenth- to fifteenth-century English that you can see in spelling,
      word inflection and grammar.
(b)   Write out the Caxton text in modern English, and describe the
      differences between the two versions.

(1) Fourteenth-century text (John of Trevisa)
(Note the use of both ⟨ʒ⟩ and ⟨g⟩. Which sound or sounds did ⟨ʒ⟩ now
represent?)

> Also Englischmen, þeyʒ hy hadde fram þe bygynnyng þre
> maner speche, Souþeron, Norþeron, and Myddel speche (in þe
> myddel of þe lond), as hy come of þre maner people of
> germania, noþeles, by commyxstion and mellyng furst wi
> Danes and afterward wiþ Normans, in menye þe contray   5
> longage ys apeyred, and som use   strange wlaffyng,
> chyteryng, harryng and garryng, grisbittyng.

(2) Fifteenth-century text (William Caxton)

> also englysshmen though they had fro the begynnyng thre
> maner speches Southern northern and myddel speche in the
> middel of the londe as they come of thre maner of people
> of Germania. Netheles by commyxtion and medlyng first
> with danes and afterward with normans In many thynges the   5
> countreye langage is appayred / ffor somme use straunge
> wlaffyng / chyteryng harryng garryng and grisbytyng /

> [wlaffyng = stammering; chyteryng = chattering;
> harryng = snarling; garryng = grating; grisbytyng =
> grinding of teeth]

Caxton's English, like Chaucer's a century before, was an educated
London dialect, which became established during the sixteenth and
seventeenth centuries as the written standard throughout the country,
so that from this time we gradually cease to be aware of the *spoken*
dialects of English.

Standard English today comes from this dialect, that of educated
speakers from the area bounded by London, Oxford, and Cambridge,
which were the centres of political and economic power and of learning,
and so the most influential. There have been some changes since, of
course, but comparatively few. The following quotation from George
Puttenham's *The Arte of English Poesie* (1589), advising writers which
forms of English to use, demonstrates how the prestige of London
English led to its adoption as the standard:

Ye shall therefore take the usuall speach of the Court,
and that of London and the shires lying about London
within lx. myles, and not much above.

The spelling system was not fully standardised until the publication
of Dr Samuel Johnson's *Dictionary* in the mid eighteenth century.

2.6 How to analyse a historical text

2.6.1 Old English

The Bible is an obvious source of study of English at different periods,
because we have translations going back to the Old English of King
Alfred's time in the late ninth century.

The short Old English texts in the preceding sections show that it
would be very difficult to read ninth-century English without learning
the language. The vocabulary, spelling and word forms are unfamiliar.

To show you a little more about the way inflections and other kinds
of changes in word form conveyed meaning, here is the beginning of the
parable of the Good Samaritan in Old English of the eleventh century,
in West Saxon, with a short explanation:

Sum man ferde fram Hierusalem to Hiericho, and becom on þa
sceaþan, þa hine bereafodon, and tintregodon hine, and
forleton him samcucene.

sum man	*some man* in the sense of *a certain man*.
ferde	the 3rd person singular, past tense, of the verb *feran*, *to go, journey*. The *-de* suffix became modern English *-ed*, the **regular past tense** ending. = '(he) journeyed'.
becom	the 3rd person singular, past tense, of the verb *becuman*, *to meet with*, which is marked by the change of **vowel** from ⟨u⟩ to ⟨o⟩ = *(he) met with*. It is the same verb as *become/became* today, but has changed in pronunciation (and therefore in spelling), and in meaning.
þa sceaþan	*þa* is literally *those*, and the following *þa* means *who*. *sceaþan*, *thieves*, is the **plural** of the noun *sceaþa*, *a thief*.
hine	means *him*, the **object** of the verb.
bereafodon	the 3rd person plural, marked by *-on*, and the past tense,

marked by -od, of the verb *bereafian* (modern *bereave/ bereft*), meaning *to deprive*; *(they) deprived (him of . . .)*. Notice the restricted meaning of the verb today.

tintregodon   the 3rd person plural and past tense of the verb *tintregian*, *to torture*.

forleton   the 3rd person plural and past tense of the verb *forlætan*, *to abandon*. Notice the change of vowel to mark past tense in this verb, not the suffix -od.

samcucene   means *half-alive*. The **prefix** *sam-* is the Latin *semi-*. The suffix -ne shows that the word is in **agreement** with *hine* = *him*. *cucu* is another form of the word *cwic*, meaning *alive*. Again notice the change of meaning in modern English *quick* (same pronunciation, but different spelling). The word still meant *living* in the phrase *the quick and the dead* in the King James Bible of 1611.

2.6.2 Middle English

If we move on another 300 years, to the late fourteenth century, we find that we can read the South Midland dialect of John Wyclif's Middle English translation as easily as we can read Chaucer's London dialect of the same period:

A man cam doun fro Jerusalem in to Jerico, and fel among theues, and thei robbiden hym, and woundiden hym, and wente awai, and leften the man half alyue.

The only significant differences from modern English are the -*en* and -*iden* suffixes on the verbs, which are the same as the Old English -*on* and -*odon* inflections, but pronounced differently. The -*en* suffix eventually disappeared completely, leaving just the -*ed* past tense suffix.

2.6.3 Early Modern English and Modern English

A detailed comparison of the complete parable in the 1611 translation (the *Authorised Version* of King James I), and in a modern version published in 1952, will show how a linguistic analysis can be used to discover facts about change at each language level: spelling, choice of vocabulary, word-forms, and grammar.

Both versions are translated from the original Greek of the New Testament. English in the sixteenth and seventeenth centuries is called **Early Modern English**. There are still important differences between

the language then and now, as you will know if you have studied any
Shakespeare plays in detail.

Exercise

Examine the spelling, the differences of vocabulary, and the structure
of words and sentences in the two versions of the parable, and describe
the differences between them.

(1) The Authorised Version

A certaine man went downe from Hierusalem to Jericho,
and fel among theeues, which stripped him of his raiment,
and wounded him, and departed, leauing him halfe dead.
And by chaunce there came downe a certaine Priest that
way, and when he saw him, he passed by on the other side.   5
And likewise a Leuite, when hee was at the place, came and
looked on him, and passed by on the other side. But a
certaine Samaritane as he iourneyed, came where he was;
and when hee saw him, hee had compassion on him, and went
to him, and bound vp his wounds, powring in oile and wine,   10
and set him on his owne beast, and brought him to an Inne,
and took care of him. And on the morrow when he departed,
hee tooke out two pence, and gaue them to the hoste, and
saide vnto him, Take care of him, and whatsoeuer thou
spendest more, when I come againe I will repay thee.   15
Which now of these three, thinkest thou, was neighbour
vnto him that fell among theeues? And he said, He that
shewed mercie on him. Then said Jesus vnto him, Goe, and
doe thou likewise.

(2) From 'The Four Gospels', translated by E.V. Rieu

A man going down from Jerusalem to Jericho fell into
the hands of brigands, who not only robbed but stripped
and wounded him, and then made off, leaving him half dead.
A priest, who happened to be going down by the same road,
saw him and passed by on the other side. In the same way   5

too a Levite, when he reached the spot and saw him, passed
by on the other side. But a Samaritan also came upon him
as he went along the road and was filled with compassion
directly he saw him. He went up to him, bandaged his
wounds, applying oil and wine, put him on his own mount,   10
and took him to an inn, where he attended to his comfort.
And in the morning he produced two shillings, gave them to
the innkeeper and said: 'Take care of him; and on my way
back I will repay you any further charges.'

    'Which of these three, do you think, proved himself a   15
neighbour to the man who fell into the brigands' hands?'

    'The one,' he replied, 'who treated him with
compassion.'

    And Jesus said to him: 'Go and do as he did.'

Commentary

(i) the Early Modern English Text
(a) Spelling: The words fall into groups, according to the spelling
conventions they observe:

(i)
certaine	Samaritaine	tooke	mercie
downe	oile	hoste	goe
halfe	owne	saide	doe
hee	Inne	againe	

Formerly, in the Middle English period, a final ⟨e⟩ on a word
would have been pronounced. It was all that was left of most of the
Old English inflectional endings. By the time of the 1611 Bible
translation, final ⟨e⟩s were no longer pronounced, but they survived
in spelling in a fairly random way, because spelling was not yet
standardised. Sometimes printers would add an ⟨e⟩ to a word to fill
up a line of type.

(ii)   Hierusalem   iourneyed   mercie

The rules for the use of ⟨i⟩, ⟨y⟩, and ⟨j⟩ were not yet fixed as in
modern spelling.

(iii)   theeues   Leuite   whatsoeuer   vnto
         leauing   gaue   vp

The distinction between the **vowel** /u/ and the **consonant** /v/ was not represented in the spelling. The letters ⟨u⟩ and ⟨v⟩ were used for both sounds. If either sound began a word, then letter ⟨v⟩ was used (vp, vnto, verily, victuals); if either sound was in the middle or at the end of a word, then letter ⟨u⟩ was used (ouer, fiue, thou, multitude).

(iv)   powring   chaunce   shewed   fel
These are single examples of other spelling conventions.

(b) Word forms: The only important differences which this text illustrates are in the forms of *thinkest* and *spendest*.

The suffix *-est* in the present tense of a verb marks the older regular use of the pronoun *thou/ thee* (2nd person singular). The verb ending shows **agreement** (or **concord**) with the pronoun. Today we use *you* whether we are addressing one or more than one person, and *thou* is being dropped out of use even in church services, where it was common until the 1970s. (The other verb inflection which is now lost was *-eth*, used with the 3rd person singular *he/ she/ it* – *he beareth, she giueth, it hath*.)

(c) Vocabulary: Some of the words are now out of date in everyday usage; they have become **archaisms**:

    raiment   likewise   hoste   etc.

There are also set phrases, **collocations**, which are no longer in current use:

    went down from   fel among   had compassion on
    on the morrow   powring in oile etc.

There is no clear boundary between features of interest in the vocabulary, and those in the grammar.

(d) Grammar: The differences between Early Modern English and present-day English grammar, apart from those in (b) above, are relatively small, but **word order** shows some contrasts:

there came down a certaine Priest
doe thou likewise
thinkest thou?

To ask a question in English today when using the simple present tense (e.g. *you think*) or simple past tense (e.g *you thought*), we have to introduce the **auxiliary verb** *do*:

do you think?   did you think?

This form of the **verb phrase** is called **interrogative mood**.

To give a command or make a direct request, we would now say, for *do thou likewise*, in which *do* is being used as a **main verb**:

go and do it   you go and do it

This form of the verb is called **imperative mood**. Notice also the very frequent use of the **conjunction** *and* to link clauses and also to begin sentences. We do this in ordinary spoken English, especially when telling a story. The 1611 version of the parable has twice as many instances of *and* as the modern version, joining clauses or beginning sentences, which makes it sound much closer to oral narrative.

(ii) The 1952 translation

(a) Spelling: Our spelling system has been standardised for over 200 years, and we only mis-spell deliberately for special reasons (for example cf. *Dialect in Literature* in chapter 9). So there is nothing to be said about the spelling of this translation. It is **standard spelling**.

(b)   Word forms: The inflections of verbs and nouns conform to the rules of **Standard English**.

(c)   Vocabulary: Any translator of the Bible into modern English must be influenced by the 1611 version, and by the formal dignity of its style. So we find words that are perhaps not frequently used in modern English, or which sound literary or formal, especially in some phrases:

fell into the hands of *brigands*
applying oil and wine

put him on his own *mount*
he *attended to* his comfort
I will repay you any *further charges*

Notice also how the translator uses the words of the King James Bible in 'leaving him half dead' and 'passed by on the other side'.

(d) Grammar: There is more variation in sentence structure and in the use of linking words between clauses than in the 1611 translation. The word *and* occurs less frequently, and the use of the **relative clause** construction, and the **non-finite verb** contributes to the variety.
Compare:

A man going down from . . .	A certaine man went down from . . .
[non-finite verb]	[main clause]
A priest, who happened . . .	And by chaunce there came down. . .
[relative clause]	[main clause]

This chapter has outlined very briefly the historical background to English. The language was brought here from the Continent 1,500 years ago. Its main word-stock is Germanic, from Old English and Old Norse; many hundreds of French words were adopted in the Middle English period. The other principal source of our vocabulary, not yet mentioned, is Latin. Many Latin words were used to coin English words by writers, especially in the sixteenth and seventeenth centuries. But if you are interested in words and where they came from, or their **etymology**, a good dictionary or history of English will show you how English speakers have adopted words from many other languages.

We have looked at some examples of older English, and shown how the differences can be described in terms of spelling, vocabulary, word-form and grammar. Old English and Middle English, like modern English, consisted of distinctive dialects, but Standard English as we know it today did not begin to emerge as the accepted *written* form of the language until the later fifteenth century. Since then, Standard English has become the ordinary spoken form of English for many people – the form discussed in chapter 1, widely thought of as 'correct English'.

The important thing to remember is that all the dialects of present-day English spoken in England, including Standard English, and the dialectal accents associated with them, including RP, are traced back directly to the dialects of Middle and Old English.

Exercise 3:

Here is a short extract from St Luke's Gospel in Middle English and
Early Modern English.
(a)   Compare the spelling, vocabulary, word structure and grammar
      with present-day Standard English. (The verses are numbered.)
(b)   Look up the origins of the words in the Early Modern English
      text and list them according to their language of origin: Old
      English, Old Norse, French or Latin.

(1) Middle English (c. 1380)

21. And thei axiden hym, and seiden, Maister, we witen,
that riȝtli thou seist and techist; and thou takist not
the persoone of man, but thou teichist in treuthe the
weie of God.
22. Is it leueful to vs to ȝyue tribute to the emperoure,   5
or nay?
23. And he biheld the disseit of hem, and seide to hem,
What tempten ȝe me?
24. Shewe ȝe to me a peny; whos ymage and superscripcioun
hath it? Thei answerden, and seiden to hym, The   10
emperouris.
25. And he seide to hem, ȝelde ȝe therfor to the emperoure
tho thingis that ben the emperours, and tho thingis that
ben of God, to God.

(2) Early Modern English (1611)

21. And they asked him, saying, Master, we know that thou
sayest and teachest rightly, neither acceptest thou the
person of any, but teachest the way of God truely.
22. Is it lawfull for vs to giue tribute vnto Cesar, or no?
23. But he perceiued their craftines, and said vnto them,   5
Why tempt ye me?
24. Shew me a peny: whose image and superscription hath it?
They answered, and said, Cesars.
25. And he said vnto them, Render therefore vnto Cesar the
things which be Cesars, and vnto God the things which be   10
Gods.

Exercise 4

Only a few of the spelling and printing conventions of the sixteenth
century have been mentioned so far. Below is a **facsimile** of part of a
modern reprint of William Tyndale's translation of *The Pentateuch* (the
first five books of the Old Testament), originally printed in 1530.

Examine it carefully and discuss the differences between the repro-
duction of Tyndale's printed English and modern printed English in
terms of letter-forms and spelling. Then look at differences in vocabulary
and grammar.

The fyrst boke of Moses, VIII. I–II

The .VIII. Chapter. [Fo. X.]

1 AND god remēbred Noe & all ỹ
beaſtes & all ỹ catell ỹ were
with hī in ỹ arke And god
made a wynde to blow vppō
2 ỹ erth, & ỹ waters ceaſed: ād ỹ fountaynes
of the depe ād the wyndowes of heavē
were ſtopte and the rayne of heaven was
3 forbiddē, and the waters returned from of
ỹ erth ād abated after the ende of an hundred and .L
dayes.

*M.C.S. Af-
ter the ſend-
yng forth of
the rauē & the
doue Noe went
forth of the
arcke. He
offreth ſacri-
fice. The
malyce of
mannes heart.*

4 And the arke reſted vppō the mountayns of Ararat,
5 the .xvii. daye of the .vii. moneth. And the waters
went away ād decreaſed vntyll the .x. moneth. And
the fyrſt daye of the tenth moneth, the toppes of the
mounteyns appered.
6 And after the ende of .XL. dayes. Noe opened the
7 wyndow of the arke which he had made, ād ſent forth
a raven, which went out, ever goinge and cominge
agayne, vntyll the waters were dreyed vpp vppon the
erth

3

Dialects and Standard English – the present

3.1 Standard English a dialect

When Chaucer wrote *The Canterbury Tales* at the end of the fourteenth century, there was no Standard English. He wrote in the educated variety of the London area, where he lived and worked. William Langland wrote *Piers Plowman* in the South Midland dialect. The York Mystery Plays were written in the Northern dialect. The poem *Sir Gawain and the Green Knight* is in the West Midland dialect of Lancashire or Cheshire. The writer John of Trevisa used a South-Western dialect.

The contrast is not as great as it may seem if we think of Standard English today as one dialect among many. The English language, then and now, consists of the sum of all its dialects, not of one correct version and a number of substandard varieties.

But even if Standard English is defined as one dialect among many, it is no longer a **regional dialect**. It has spread throughout the world as the educated variety of English, so it is natural that people should come to look on the other dialects as imperfect versions of English. To the linguist, however, all dialects of English are equally regular in their own forms and rules.

Dialect words can, of course, fail to convey their meaning if they are unfamiliar to a listener. The number of words still regularly used in dialects, and which are not part of the vocabulary of Standard English, is much smaller now than a generation or two ago. Easier travel, people moving from one area to another, the influence of film, radio and television, and the effects of over a century of compulsory education, will all have influenced the vocabulary of dialects. Almost everyone can now hear Standard English, in a wide variety of its styles, every day, and a large amount of American English also. But in spite of the loss of dialect words, there is plenty of evidence of dialectal grammar.

41

3.2 Present-day dialectal forms

The most noticeable differences between present-day dialects and Standard English in England lie in quite a small set of grammatical features, illustrated in the sentences below. Some of them were included in the *Acceptability Test* in chapter 1.

Exercise 1

Before reading the commentary which follows the dialectal sentences, identify and describe the words or constructions which are **non-standard**.

Are any of the sentences difficult to understand? If so, can you say why?

1. I didn't have no dinner yesterday.
2. My Dad seen an accident before he come home the other day.
3. My sister have a boy friend and she see him every day.
4. That was the man what done it.
5. John fell over and hurt hisself.
6. Mary's more nicer than her brother.
7. She spoke very clever.
8. Leave your things here while you come back.
9. Our teacher can't learn us anything.
10a. I want this coat cleaning. OR This coat needs cleaning.
10b. I want this coat cleaned. OR This coat needs cleaned.
11. She gave it her friend.
12a. I were going down the road.
12b. We was going down the road.
13. If you're tired, why don't you lay down?
14. The water was dripping out the tap.
15. Will you go and buy me two pound of apples?
16. You can gan out to play now.
17. We never had TV them days when I were a lad.
18. She wanted for to go till visit her mother.

Commentary

In these sentences the dialectal forms are not identified as belonging to any particular region of England. They are all genuine, but many of them are widespread. They illustrate variations in the grammar of English which we can place together as non-standard. You would expect them to be spoken with a dialectal accent also, but this is being treated as a separate topic for study.

One of the purposes of this book is to encourage you to listen to varieties of English speech objectively. You should learn to identify the differences accurately, taking Standard English as the norm for vocabularly and grammar. Whether you like a particular dialect or accent is not relevant.

1. I didn't have no dinner yesterday (cf. Acceptability Test no. 8)

If spoken in a normal way, it means the same as Standard English 'I didn't have any dinner yesterday', or more formally, 'I had no dinner yesterday'. That is:

/I didn't have no dinner yesterday/

It is not true that two negatives necessarily make a positive in language, although they do in mathematics. Many languages make more than one item negative in a sentence; Old English and Middle English did, which is where the present-day dialects that use the **double** or **multiple negative** get it from. Standard English has changed. Here are some examples:

Old English (the negative word was *ne*, before the verb)

    ne þurfan ge *noht* besorgian

= *ne* need you *not* fear

= you need *not* fear

    (the word *noht* reinforces the negative *ne*, and is the origin of modern English *not*)

Middle English (from the *Peterborough Chronicle* for 1137)

    for *ne* wæren *nævre nan* martyrs swa pined alse hi wæron

= for *never* were*n't no* martyrs so tortured as they were

= for *never* were martyrs tortured as they were (Standard English)

The multiple negative in present-day dialects is therefore a survival of older forms of the language, not badly learned Standard English.

In certain other linguistic constructions, however, two negatives do make a positive. The *Oxford English Dictionary* records its first example from 1657:

The study of antiquity was *not un*usefull . . .

The use of *not* with an adjective or adverb which has a negative prefix is still quite common, though usually in a formal style. But this is not the same construction as the preceding examples from Old and Middle English and dialects.

It is possible to speak sentence 1 in such a way as to imply the positive, by using **contrastive stress**:

/I didn't have **nŏ** dinner yésterday/

But this is quite clearly different from the unmarked normal **intonation** pattern which implies the negative, and is in everyday use in many English dialects.

2. My Dad seen an accident before he come home the other day
Standard English would have *saw* and *came*, the **simple past tense** of *see* and *come*.

The **regular past tense** in English consists of the **base form** of a verb, e.g. *walk*, to which the suffix *-ed* is added in writing. (The pronunciation varies, but will not be discussed here.)

She *walked* to the station to meet me.

The form of the verb called the **past participle** is exactly the same as the past tense in regular verbs. Together with *have* it forms the **present perfect** tense:

She *has walked* to the station every day.

or the **past perfect** tense:

She *had walked* to the station every day.

There is, however, a large set of **irregular** verbs, most of them very common, whose past tenses and past participles are not formed by adding *-ed*. These irregular verbs are in fact the oldest in form, going back beyond Old English in time to Germanic, and finally to the language from which most European languages have developed, called **Indo-European**. As a result, they tend to resist change. Grammarians have called them **strong verbs**, and the regular verbs **weak**.

So our modern irregular verbs are the remnant of the Old English strong verbs, and show a variety of different kinds of change in their forms. Here are a few examples:

(a) One form only:

base form	past tense	past participle
let	let	let

In this group of verbs, the base form, and therefore the present tense also, is the same as the past tense and past participle:

I *let* him go there whenever he wants to.
I *let* him go there yesterday.
I *have let* him go, although I didn't want to.

Type (a) is a group of verbs which have lost the distinction between base form, past, and past participle forms. There is only one form. Compare *cost, hit, hurt, put, set, shut, spread*, etc.

(b) Two forms:

(i)	swing	swung	swung
(ii)	come	came	come

Type (b) verbs have two forms. In b(i) the past tense and past participle have 'fallen together', taking the form of the OE past participle. Type b(ii) has the same form for the base/present tense and past participle.

(c) Three forms:

see	saw	seen
do	did	done

Type (c) verbs have three forms. The past tense and past participle are different from each other and from the base/present tense form.

The changes that took place in verb forms between the Old English and Middle English periods, and then further changes up to today, are very complicated. Different changes took place in each of the different dialects, and so survive into modern dialects. The examples given above all show Standard English forms, but many dialect verbs are non-standard in form.

In the dialects represented in sentence (2), the past tense and past participle of *see* have fallen together, both taking the form of the past participle as in standard type b(i) above:

I see   I seen   I have seen

In the verb *come*, the same thing has happened, but since the past participle had the same root vowel as the infinitive in Old English (c*u*men/ c*u*man), these dialects have the same vowel for all three forms, like Type (a) in Standard English:

I come   I come   I have come

The important point that this rather detailed description shows is, that though at first the dialectal forms sound wrong if you are used to Standard English, they can be explained linguistically in exactly the same way as Standard English forms. It is simply that different choices were made among the varied **speech communities** forming the speakers of English in the past. These choices are not conscious or deliberate, but pronunciation is always changing, and leads in time to changes in word form.

3.   *My sister have a boy friend and she see him every day*
Standard English is *has* and *sees*. The present tense of verbs uses the base form, except that the 3rd person singular adds an -*s*:

I see	I have
he sees	she has
they see	they have
you see	you have

Dialects using the base form for the 3rd person singular, and not adding the -*s*, have taken to its conclusion the process of simplifying the forms of the present tense. Standard English and other dialect speakers have not taken this step.

4.   *That was the man what done it*

Two non-standard features, *done* for *did* (past tense) and *what* for *who* or *that*:

That was the man who did it.

The use of *done* for the past tense is another example of the alternative forms described for sentence 2.

What has a number of functions in Standard English, and it is not surprising that its use in some dialects overlaps with that of other **pronouns** like *that*, *which*, and *who*. In this sentence it is functioning as the **relative pronoun**.

	Standard	*Dialectal*
	The woman who came. . .	The woman what came. . .
	The man who I saw. . .	The man what I saw
or	The man whom I saw. . .	
	The girl that called. . .	The girl what called. . .
	The pen which he gave. . .	The pen what he gave. . .
or	The pen that he gave. . .	

In some dialects, *as* is used as the relative pronoun:

The chap as called last night was an old friend.

5.   *John fell over and hurt hisself*

The standard form is *himself*. Why? Look at the following lists of **personal pronouns**:

me	my	meself	**myself**
him	his	**himself**	hisself*
her	her	**herself**	**herself**
it	its	**itself**	**itself**
us	our	usselves	**ourselves**
you	your	youselves	**yourselves**
them	their	**themselves**	theirselves*

Standard English uses *my/our/your* + *self/selves*, but not *his/their*, and there seems to be no logical reason why.

> *me/him* etc. are **object pronouns**:
> He saw *me*.   I saw *him*.

> *my/his* etc. are **possessive pronouns**:
> This is *my* bike.   That's *his* bike.

Dialects using *hisself* and *theirselves* are consistently using the *possessive pronoun* + *self/selves* to form the **reflexive pronoun**, and Standard English is here inconsistent.

6.   *Mary's more nicer than her brother*
We form the **comparative** of an adjective either by adding the suffix *-er*, or by using *more* + the adjective, in Standard English.

> She is *nicer* than he is.
> She is *more intelligent* than he is.

The 'double comparative' is a feature of some dialects, similar in some ways to the double negative.

7.   *She spoke very clever*
In Standard English the **adverb** form is *cleverly*. Most adverbs in English today end in *-ly*. A few common ones derive from Old English adverbs, some of which ended in the suffix *-e*, which was then pronounced as a syllable. This suffix has now disappeared, leaving some adverbs without one:

> The car was stuck *fast* in the mud.
> Open the window *wide*.

The word *clever* was not an Old English adverb, but if some adverbs don't end in *-ly*, it is possible that other adverbs drop the suffix by **analogy**, or imitation. Analogy helps to explain many changes in word forms.

8.   Leave your things here while you come back
If you do not live in the North of England, you may never have heard this use of *while*. The standard form is:

Leave your things here until you come back.

It is said that the first notices placed at unmanned level crossings, when they were first introduced, stated:

Wait while lights flash

Since this means, for some dialect speakers,

Wait until lights flash

you can see how dangerous the notice was.
    If you ask someone in a shop what their opening hours are, they might reply:

We're open from nine in the morning while five in the afternoon.

9.   Our teacher can't learn us anything
In Standard English, *to learn* means *to acquire knowledge*. In some dialects, it also means *to impart knowledge*. How can one word have two opposite meanings?
    This is not so unusual as you might at first think. For example:

I *rent* a flat *from* a landlord.
The landlord *rents* a flat *to* me.

and so:

He *learned* it *from* me.
I *learned* it *to* him.

To learn comes from an Old English verb *leornian*, and its meaning in the sense of *to impart* and *to acquire* knowledge is recorded in writing, and therefore in educated usage, up to the nineteenth century. It is only recently that the meaning equivalent to *to teach* has become non-standard, but it survives in spoken English in many dialects.

Here are some examples of its use, meaning *to teach*, taken from the *Oxford English Dictionary*:

1382   Who lerneth a scornere, doth wrong he to
      himself. (Wyclif's Bible)
1535   Lede me in thy trueth and lerne me. (Coverdale's Bible)
1666   That my Father might learn me to speak without
      this wicked way of swearing. (Bunyan)
1893   My father learned it to me. (Robert Louis Stevenson)

10.   I want this coat cleaning. This coat needs cleaning. I want this coat cleaned. This coat needs cleaned
These forms are all in common use, but in different parts of Britain. The standard forms are probably 'This coat needs cleaning', and 'I want this coat cleaned', but perhaps it is a matter of stylistic variation.

11.   She gave it her friend
Standard usage would require either:

      She gave it to her friend.
or   She gave her friend it.

We are here talking about the **direct object** and **indirect object** of the verb. *To give* implies something which she gave (the direct object, DO), and person to whom she gave it (the indirect object, IO).
She gave <u>her friend</u> a <u>birthday present</u>.

        IO   DO

She gave <u>a birthday present</u> <u>to her friend</u>.

        DO   *prepositional object*

The term *indirect object* is best reserved for the form without the preposition *to*, and in Standard English and most other dialects it precedes the direct object.
   If a **prepositional phrase** with *to* (or *for*) is used, then it follows the direct object. But if pronouns are used instead of nouns, the meaning can be slightly confusing:

She gave him it.   She gave it him.
She gave her friend it.   She gave it her friend.

Both pairs seem acceptable, because common sense tells us that it is unlikely that she would give a person (*him*/ *her friend*) to a thing (*it*), and the meaning 'She gave him to it' is less probable. In any case, the sentence would be spoken in a context in which the referents of *him* and *it* were known.

12. I were going down the road. We was going down the road
Standard English conjugates the verb *to be* in the past tense as follows:

I/he/she/it *was*   we/you/they *were*

This is more or less as it was in Old English:

ic/he/heo/hit *wæs*   we/ge/hi *wæron* & þu *wære*

but many dialects have brought the past tense of *to be* in line with all other verbs, which have only *one* form for the past tense. Some dialects have regularised the past tense to *was*, others to *were*. They are not muddling their usage, but simplifying it. The two sentences in 12 are not from the same dialect.

13. If you're tired, why don't you lay down?
A favourite mistake for teachers to mark wrong, but still a common usage. Standard English distinguishes two verbs:

to lie   I lie (present)   I lay (past)
to lay   I lay (present)   I laid (past)

The past tense of *lie* has the same form as the base and present tense form of *lay*, so the confusion is easy to understand.

But the use of *lay* meaning *lie* was common in written English, and not regarded as a **solecism** (bad grammar) until the nineteenth century.

   c. 1300 Sathanas, y bynde the, her shalt thou lay.
         (a mystery play, *The Harrowing of Hell*)
     1625 Nature will lay buried a great time, and yet revive.
         (Francis Bacon's essay *On Nature*)
     1818 Thou dashest him again to earth, there let him lay.
         (Byron)

In grammatical terms, Standard English *lie* is **intransitive** and is not followed by a direct object – you can't *lie something* – while *lay* is **transitive** and is followed by an object – you can *lay the table*, and hens *lay eggs*. Some dialects use *lay* as an intransitive verb.

14.   *The water was dripping out the tap*
Standard English *out of*. Variation in the use of **prepositions** is widespread between the dialects of English, including the standard. Prepositions can be simple (one word) or complex (two or more words), and the possible combinations allow many variations. For example:

along	along with	away	away from
off	off of	together	together with
by means of	on top of	in front of	in relation to

15.   *Will you buy me two pound of apples?*
This is very common. You might expect the plural form *pounds*, as the word *two* means more than one. There are, however, many **noun phrases** of measurement in which the noun remains singular. For example:

I walked three mile into town.

This may possibly be a direct descendant from the Old English, when *three miles wide* would have been þreora mila brad which is literally *of three miles broad*. *Two pounds* was *twegen punda*, literally *two of pounds*.

In Old English, as we have already seen, words were inflected to show their grammatical relationships in a phrase or sentence. Modern English tends to use prepositions, or word order, for the same purpose.

The words for *of miles* and *of pounds* in expression of measurement in Old English were *mila* and *punda*. (The *-a* inflection marks the **possessive plural** form.) These words eventually became *mile* and *pound* because the ending was dropped, and some dialects still use this grammatical form without the *-s* plural.

It is quite usual in Standard English to say 'He's six *foot* tall', and to talk of a 'three-*foot* ruler'. The Old English form was *syx fota*. This is another example of the dialects retaining older features of the language.

16.   You can gan out to play now
The Old English verb for *go* was *gan*. The vowel /ɑ/ was a long vowel, and *gan* changed to *gon* in early Middle English, in the south of England, and later lost the final /n/ to become *go*.

This change did not occur in the north, and *gan* is still common in the North-East of England.

17.   We never had TV them days when I were a lad
Non-standard features are the use of *never* for the negative 'We didn't have TV. . .', the use of *them* for the **demonstrative pronoun** *those*, and the omission of a preposition before *them days - in those days*.

The use of *never* may not be accepted as dialectal, but as an **informal** feature of Standard English grammar also. Dialects and styles do not have fixed definable boundaries.

I were has already been discussed.

18.   She wanted for to go till visit her mother
For occurs with *to* in Standard English in constructions like:

For me *to* understand this is easy.
What he wants is *for* her *to* visit her mother.
The idea is *for* him *to* go next week.

Some dialects retain both *for* and *to* in construction where Standard English omits *for*:

I want *for to* go Widecombe Fair.

The use of *till* where most dialects and standard English use *to* is a survival from Old English, when the word for *to* was *til*.

These examples of non-standard dialect illustrate some of the principal differences between Standard English and the dialects today, most of them from England. It is not a complete list, but because the differences in word-form and grammar are much less marked now than in previous centuries, it represents some of the most common differences. Because we are sensitive to even small changes in word-form or grammar, our judgements of a dialect speaker may rest upon very few items of difference.

The detailed linguistic commentary on the dialectal sentences has been done for two reasons:

(i)   to show you how to make an objective analysis of a piece of language before you go on to evaluate it, and

(ii)   to illustrate the fact that Standard English is just as arbitrary in its choice of words and structures as other dialects and languages.

Exercise 2

The following sentences are from Sir Thomas Malory's *Le Morte Darthur*, and they illustrate the form of literary English of 500 years ago which was to become Standard English. The book was printed by Caxton in 1485.

Identify those features which are nowadays regarded as non-standard or dialectal, and relate them to the dialectal sentences of Exercise 1:

1. And in the meanewhyle I and my sistir woll ryde untyll your castell.
2. His castell is here nerehonde but two myle.
3. But in no wyse I wolde nat that he wyste what I were.
4. Than was syr Gareth more gladder than he was tofore.
5. Hit was never done by me, nother by myne assente this unhappy dede was never done.
6. Ryght so come this damesell Lyonett before hem all.
7. For such yonge knyghtes as he is, whan they be in their adventures, bene never abydyng in no place.
8. We shall be full sore macched with the moste nobleste knyghtes of the worlde.
9. And than sir Trystrams and his bretherne rode togydyrs for to helpe sir Gareth.
10. If I may nat have hym, I promyse you I woll never have none.

Exercise 3

Compare the following descriptive definitions of Standard English:

(a)   'Standard English is... "normal English"; that kind of English which draws least attention to itself over the widest area and through the widest range of usage. 'It is particularly associated with English in a *written form*, and we find that there are sharper restrictions in every way upon the English that is written (and especially *printed*) than upon English that is spoken.' (Randolph Quirk, *The Use of English*, 1962)

(b)   'The *Standard* is that speech variety of a language community which is legitimised as the obligatory norm for social intercourse on the strength of the interests of dominant forces in that society.' (Norbert Dittmar, *Sociolinguistics*, 1976)

Exercise 4

The following sentences are authentic examples of contemporary speech. Identify and describe the dialectal features. Some of them have not been discussed in this chapter. (Cassette tape, Section 3)

1.   If she know she got it coming cushy she ain't got to bother, have she? (Berkshire)
2.   I seed the advertisement in the newspaper and our Dad said to I, 'If thee carsn't do that as good as some of the men, that's a poor job'. (Gloucestershire)
3.   All them men had all to get motor transport for to get till it, and come in their own cars and one thing and another, so there must be something in a drum for all them people for to go for to hear them drums. (Belfast)
4.   And there were never a betterer mental arithmetic reckoner than my father, but not with a pen. Well, he could set 'em down, but not write letters, nor my mother couldn't - not till I got big enough - even write her name, and we learned her to just write it, and that were all they could do them days. (West Yorkshire)
5.   We used to have cookers out there and everything, and we used to cook our trotters there – all come up in trays, all jelly – they used to nosh 'em there like. It was really beautiful. (London)
6.   One of the teachers, the teacher what I had last - I were only about five and I were staying to school dinners - and she made me eat a big load of mashed potatoes. (Lancashire)
7.   I was sitting here writing a letter to dear Willie's mother. Her's up to Brent, her was working but now her of course has gone. And I was blowed right up there. (Devon)
8.   I'm not sprucing you. They knew every kid in the village, and if they come through the village and they see you, they always used to call you 'master', and you always used to touch your cap and call them 'sir'. (Sussex)

9.   A good boss was a good boss. He were paying for the stuff that I
     were supposed to make perfect or as near perfect as possible. It's
     his money. It's his building. It's all that. He's kept your childer
     for so many year. Well you work for him, style of thing – hasn't
     he? (Lancashire)

10. I usually just sub, but then again, I'm a defender. I likes playing
     defender more than anything else. (Plymouth)

11. I used to work in Marks and Spencer's. We've always kept friends
     with the people in there, you know. And then I worked on the
     station for nineteen year. (Carlisle)

12. When I heard the knocking I never thought nothing like that
     could ever happen. (Norwich)

3.3   Creole English

During the last 30 years, new dialects have appeared in England which
were formerly to be heard only in the dominions and colonies of the
former British Empire. Families who emigrated from the West Indies to
Britain in the 1950s and 1960s found that although they spoke English,
it was different in many ways from the English they heard in Britain.
Their language had developed from the early days of slavery in the West
Indies, as far back as the seventeenth century, when a simplified form
of English – a **pidgin** – was used for giving orders and communicating. A
pidgin language is a **contact language** which develops and is used by two
sets of people when neither knows the other's language. A pidgin may
in time develop into a first language, or **mother tongue**. Linguists then
call it a **creole**. A creole, like any other first language, grows to serve all
the purposes of language in a society.

   Some of the differences between a West Indian creole and other
forms of English can be heard in the following story told by a small boy
who had recently come to live in England. This first transcription is not
edited, and includes the hesitations and self-corrections which the boy
makes, because some of them are significant clues to his knowledge of
English. Ordinary spelling is used, and pronunciation and intonation are
not indicated. Momentary breaks are marked with the sign (.)

Exercise 1

Listen to the cassette tape recording and follow the transcription. Then make a list of all the non-standard features in vocabulary, word-form and grammar, together with the Standard English equivalents.

(1) THE MANGO TREE   *Cassette tape Section 4*

every night we don't go to bed soon and in the morning
(when) we wake up soon and we race one another to go to
the mango tree (.) and every morning my big brother always
racing me and get more mango than me
when we have a mango we don't carry it down (.) because   5
you know (.) when we go to school them other will eat it
off and when we come from school in the evening we go for
them and eat them
and always my granma (.) my granma (.) when we hided (.)
the mango in the ground he (.) he (.) she always find it (.)   10
and eat them off and when we go and look for them
there was none mango but the seed and the skin
and when we come down and ask where (.) where (.) where
the mango we cannot have ..? .. (.) and my granny say he
(.) she eat them off and she say you (.) we mustn't   15
hide no more in the ground (.) and (.) in the grass we
hide them and he still find them
one morning I find one dozen mango and I hide them in
the bush and my brother come (.) run home soon and come
and eat them off and I didn't get none (.) and I tell my   20
granny and sh.(.) and I tell my granny and he beat him
[*teacher*: she beat your brother?] yes (.) he say she
**mustn't eat off the mangoes and me don't get any (.) and
she tell him to stop it**
every time when my granny beat him always my dog (.) my   25
dog come in and bark at him (.) and he lick after the dog
and the dog run away

Commentary

This is a simple narrative typical, in its structure, of any young child's story-telling with its succession of clauses linked by *and* and *when*. The non-standard features must be grouped into sets in order to explain them:

(i) Tense

Is the boy telling his story in the present tense, which is common enough in oral narrative, or in the past tense? In Standard English, we use the **base form** of a verb for the **infinitive**, e.g. *to come*, and for the **present tense**, except for the 3rd person singular, with *he/she/it*, which has an *-s* added:

> I, we, you, they *come* / she *comes*

For the **past tense** we either change the vowel of the verb:

> I, he, we, you, they *came*

or we add *-ed*:

> I, it, we, you, they *raced*

All the verbs used by the boy are in the base form, except for the single use of *hided*. In creole English, verbs are not inflected to show present or past tense, just like a small set of verbs in Standard English already discussed (see section 3.2, page 45), neither does the 3rd person singular verb take an *-s*.

This does not mean that you cannot tell past from present in creole, but that you don't do so by inflecting the verb. If necessary, you use a separate word, like *did* or *been*. Different dialects of a language, like different languages, convey similar meanings but in different ways. Some dialects are more developed and complex than others, as is Standard English compared with creoles of English. It can be assumed therefore that the boy's narrative is in the past tense.

(ii) Nouns

A second set of differences is in the form of the **nouns**, e.g. *mango* for *mangoes* (except once). Creoles do not mark nouns for plural. Standard English nouns usually inflect with an *-s*, but there are a few with **zero plural**: e.g. *sheep / salmon / deer / grouse*, so creole usage is not altogether different.

(iii) Gender

Thirdly, there is, to us, confusion in the boy's use of *he/ she/ him/ her*.

He hesitates when he wants to refer to his granny, and gets the pronouns wrong: 'and I tell my granny and he beat him'.

Standard English distinguishes **masculine**, **feminine** and **neuter gender** in the singular 3rd person pronouns:

he, him, his / she, her, her / it, it, its

Creoles do not mark 3rd person singular pronouns for gender, just as Standard English does not mark any other pronouns for gender. This probably explains the boy's confusion. He has not been in England very long, but he is already using *he* and *she*, *him* and *her*, and sometimes getting them wrong from our point of view.

These are the three main differences between the grammar of the boy's English and Standard English. Notice the double negatives. The small differences of vocabulary do not cause any problems of understanding – *soon* for *early*, *eat off* for *eat up*, and *lick after* for *run after*.

Remember that creoles and other dialects are all rule-governed varieties of a language, internally consistent. A creole speaker learning to use another dialect is bound to mix up the two sets of rules. According to the social situation, an English dialect speaker will often use both dialectal and standard forms during the same conversation. So we heard the boy using *mangoes* once, and *hided*, and he got *she* right most of the time.

The following story is told by a small girl who had come to England from the West Indies. It gives a fascinating insight into a way of life in which a belief in ghosts and the supernatural is commonplace. She is using a mixture of creole and standard forms.

Exercise 2

Listen to the tape recording, and write down the words you hear to fill in the blank spaces in the following transcription. One of your problems will be to decide whether or not you can hear the *-ed* past tense inflection on some verbs, and the *-s* inflection for plural or possessive on nouns.

Having identified what you think the girl said, list her non-standard forms and their standard equivalents. Then describe her use of both creole and standard forms under these headings:

1. use of the base form of the verb and inflected past tense forms.
2. use of the verb *be* as a linking verb.
3. use of double negatives.
4. use of plural inflections on nouns
5. use of possessive inflections on nouns.
6. use of pronouns marked for gender.
7. unfamiliar vocabulary.

(2)   THE RED BIRD   *Cassette tape Section 5*

once upon a time there was a man . .1. . Mr Lenny Campbell
his wife . . 2 . .
and one day my brother . . 3 . . (.) and he . . 4 . . a big bird
up on the tree
it was a red bird   5
and then he . . 5 . . his catapult and . . 6 . . to . . 7 . . it
Alec . . 8 . . to . . 9 . . it
and when he . . 10 . . to . . 11 . . it [*sentence not completed*]
when he . . 12 . . the bird off the tree (.) his hand . . 13 . .
right behind his back   10
and he couldn't . . 14 . . back from his back
he . . 15 . . to pull it from his back but he couldn't
and so he . . 16 . . to Mr Lenny Campbell (.) and Mr Lenny
Campbell . . 17 . . 'what can I do about it?'
and he . . 18 . . 'I cannot do . . 19 . . about it so you'd better   15
. . 20 . . to your granny at once and . . 21 . . her before your
hands all . . 22 . . together'
and so my brother . . 23 . . (.) and when he . . 24 . . to my
granny (.) my granny . . 25 . . 'what have you been . . 26 . .
with your . . 27 . .?'   ·   20
and he said 'I . . 28 . . just shooting a bright bird off the
tree (.) a red one (.) and then my . . 29 . . . . . . 30 . . behind
me'
and so my granny . . 31 . . 'all right (.) come on'
and she . . 32 . . me to the shop(.) to go and get two . . 33 . .   25
of corn meal
and I . . 34 . . to get it (.) and some bana-bush
and she . . 35 . . it and she . . 36 . . all around the . . 37 . . (.)
and . . 38 . . it all over his . . 39 . .
and then the next morning it . . 40 . . too bad (.) but he   30

could hardly move his . . 41 . .
and then my granny . . 42 . . him to go outside and stand up
by the same tree again and try and get a catapult and
throw [*sentence not completed*]
and there would be another bird and he must . . 43 . . after   35
it
but there wasn't a bird (.) it was the ghost (.) it was Mr
Lenny . . 44 . . . . 45 . . ghost
she . . 46 . . (.) and she didn't have a peaceful place to
rest (.) so she was all around the place (.) and she   40
. . 47 . . everything to try and kill . . 48 . . husband

3.4   Pidgin English

Most pidgin languages are spoken only, but sometimes a pidgin is used
as an official language, and a writing system is invented for its spelling,
for example in Papua New Guinea.

In Vanuatu (the former New Hebrides islands in the Pacific), which
was administered as a 'condominium' by Great Britain and France until
1980, when independence was achieved, the pidgin language Bislama is
used as a common language, or **lingua franca**. Among about 100,000
people, there are 115 languages still in use, so Bislama is useful for
Vanuatuans to communicate with each other.

A written system using the Roman alphabet was devised for a translation of the New Testament published in the 1970s, based on **phonemic**
principles – that is, one letter representing one sound – so you must not
expect to be able to recognise words by just looking at them. You must
try to hear them, as if you were reading a phonetic script, and then you
will probably understand them.

Most of the vocabulary of Bislama is derived from English. Here is a
short news report from the former *New Hebrides News*, firstly in
Bislama, secondly in a literal word-for-word translation, using the
original English words, and thirdly in a modern English version. The
grammar of Bislama is not that of English. This applies especially to
the common word *i* and a suffix *-em/-im*. Try to work out what the
word and suffix are for, and also to describe some of the other grammatical features of Bislama which differ from English.

HEMI FAERAP MO I SEKEM AELAN!!

1. I kat wanfala samting we i foldaon long Sarere moning Jun 17 bitwin Merelava mo Gaua.
2. Olgeta pipol long Merelava oli talem se olgeta i lukim samting i foldaon from skae mo i kat faea bihaen long tel blong hem.
3. Taem i kasem solwora hemi faerap.
4. Olgeta i ting se hemi bom sipos nomo volkeno blong Gaua.

HIM I-FIRE-UP MORE I-SHAKE-HIM ISLAND!!

1. i-got one-fellow something that i-fall down along Saturday morning June 17 between Merelava more Gaua.
2. Altogether people along Merelava all-i-tell-him say altogether i-look-him something i-fall down from sky more i-got fire behind along tail belong him.
3. Time i-catch-him saltwater him i-fire up.
4. Altogether i-think say him i-bomb suppose no more volcano belong Gaua.

EXPLOSION SHAKES ISLAND!!

1. There was something that fell between Merelava and Gaua on Saturday morning June 17th.
2. All the people on Merelava reported (that) they saw something fall from the sky and there was fire behind in its tail (= and it had a tail of fire).
3. When it hit the sea it exploded.
4. They thought it was a bomb or else a volcano on Gaua.

And to conclude, here is the Lord's Prayer from the New Testament (St Matthew's Gospel, chapter 6, verses 9 to 13) in Bislama:

Papa bilong mifala, yu yu stap antap long heven,
Mifala i wantem we nem bilong yu i tabu.
Mifala i wantem we kingdom bilong yu i kam,
Mo we olgeta man long wol oli wokem olgeta samting we yu
yu wantem, olsem olgeta long heven oli stap wokem.   5
Mifala i askem yu bilong tedei yu givem kakai long mifala,
i stret bilong tedei nomo.
Mifala i askem yu bilong yu fogivem mifala from ol samting
nogud bilong mifala,
Olsem we mifala i stap fogivem ol man we oli stap mekem i   10

nogud long mifala.
Mifala i askem yu bilong yu no tekem mifala i go long sam
samting we bambae oli traem mifala tumas,
Mo bilong yu blokem Setan i no kam kasem mifala.

Glossary of words that may be difficult to understand:

blong and *long* are the only two prepositions in Bislama, so use the most appropriate English preposition to translate them.
mifala (me-fellow): we / us
stap (stop): *live*, or indicates **progressive aspect** on the verb
we: that
nem: name
kam: come
mo (more): and
olgeta (altogether): all
wol: world
wokem: work
oslem (all same): just as
kakai: food
stret (straight): means something like *as it should be*
nomo (no more): only
bambae (by and by): indicates the future, *will*
traem (try); in the sense of *test*
tumas: too much
blokem (block): prevent
kasem: catch
N.B.   *i* is a grammatical predicate marker, that is, it precedes the predicate of each clause. There is no equivalent in English, and it cannot be translated.
-em/-im are verb suffixes which mark transitive verbs.

4

Regional accents and Received Pronunciation

4.1 The difference between dialect and accent

When people talk about regional English, they often use the words *accent* and *dialect* rather loosely and interchangeably. For example, they could say of someone, 'She has a broad Northern accent' or 'She speaks a strong Northern dialect', and both statements might be understood as meaning more or less the same thing. The linguistic distinction between accent and dialect has already been referred to in previous chapters: the term *accent* (sometimes *dialectal accent*) refers only to the system of pronunciation a speaker uses; *dialect* refers to a speaker's grammar and vocabulary.

In this chapter a method for analysing and comparing accents will be demonstrated, which you can use for describing other samples of regional English not represented here.

Exercise 1

On section 6 of the cassette tape, Mrs Amy Cook from the village of Wotton-under-Edge in Gloucestershire is interviewed about her work. A transcription of the interview is printed below.

Listen to the recording twice, noting down the features of Mrs Cook's speech that give away her regional origins. Unless you came from Gloucestershire, you probably would not be able to place the speaker in a particular village or even in the county. But you would be able to identify her as coming from somewhere in the South-West of England.

Answer the question, 'What is it about Mrs Cook's speech that marks her out as a West Country person?

(The interviewer's questions are not transcribed)

well for a start call me Ame (.) everybody else do . . .
I'm the only one (.) in the whole of Gloucestershire (.)
after twenty six year (.) nineteen thirty nine when war
broke out I seed the advertisement in the newspaper (.)
and our dad said to I well he said if thee carsn't do   5
that as good as some of the men he said that's a poor job
(.) well I thought myself well I wouldn't let the old man down so
I had a go (.) that's nineteen thirty nine (.) and I'm
still going strong . . .
well it was on account of the money (.) they was paying   10
(.) they was paying more for an hour than what I was
getting where I (.) was before . . .
all sorts sk. it's (.) it's got grass-cutting to do (.) in
the winter put down the grit (.) it's got siding (.)
channeling (.) I've even put up signposts . . . even put up   15
signposts . . .
no (.) I er I'm classed as a roadworker (.) I do all the
jobs all (.) all but the manual labour which is carried
out by the men . . .
all round Hutton (.) Coombe (.) Sinnel (.) Blackwaters and er   20
all round Worlds End Lane and up Sinnel Lane again and
that's my worst piece on my area is Sinnel Lane (.) all
the fish and chip paper is chucked up the bank and the
kids is on the top of the lane scorting the bloody stones
down (.) and it ain't a bit of good to sweep it up because   25
it's just as bad in ten minutes after . . .
they do (.) and it ain't no good to have litter baskets
. . .
not a bit of good (.) and it ain't no good to tell them
(.) cos they'll they'll say all right to thee face and   30
behind thee back there's (.) b. and we's just as bad as
ever . . .
well (.) take them on the average and they been't too bad (.)
but still there's (.) there's ways (.) and way (.) means
for improvement . . .   35
oh toffee papers sweet papers lollipops (.) there's sticks
(.) all the ruddy lot . . .
all on it (.) you can get barrowfuls . . .

no er (.) not in the least (.) you er you can meet all
sorts in the course of a day (.) some'll say good morning   40
Ame some'll say good night some'll say good old Ame and
some do say different . . .
oh some do say good old Ame (.) some do say bugger her . . .
no not at all (.) no cos the. there's cars is going by all
day (.) kick up a heck of dust (.) well it's a mystery   45
to I in all these years I haven't had my beauty spoiled
. . .
it is . . .
well if you (.) you see the dust I do get . . .

Commentary

Pronunciation belongs to a different **level** of language from vocabulary
and grammar. You will have discovered features from all three levels in
the tape and transcription.

Some will be **phonological**, that is, to do with the way the speaker
pronounces vowels and consonants, and with the rhythm and pitch of
her speech. It is these features which, together, make up her Gloucestershire **accent**.

Other features you will have noted are to do with the particular
words she uses (vocabulary or **lexis**), the endings she gives to words like
nouns and verbs and the way she combines words together to form
sentences (**grammar**). These lexical and grammatical features form the
basis of Mrs Cook's West Country **dialect**.

Exercise 2

List any dialect words in the transcription, and say what you think
they mean.

Exercise 3

List the features of dialectal grammar in the transcription, giving the
Standard English equivalent and identifying the differences in the way
shown in chapter 3.

4.2   Accent

Exercise 1

(a)   Attempt a description of Mrs Cook's accent, using the 26 symbols of the Roman alphabet to write down her pronunciation of vowels and consonants.

(b)   Comment on her use of intonation, or speech melody.

Commentary

It is necessary to differentiate between the two aspects of pronunciation mentioned in Exercise 1. Some of the features which mark Mrs Cook as coming from Gloucestershire are **segmental**, that is, they are to do with the way she produces the individual sound-segments from which speech is made up, already referred to as **vowels** and **consonants**.

Other features are the speed (or **tempo**) and **rhythm** of her delivery, the placement of **stress**, and the fluctuations in the **pitch** and **loudness** of her voice. These are said to be 'overlaid upon' her speech, and so are called **supra-segmental**. Another term for them is **prosodic** features.

(i) Supra-segmental features
The supra-segmental aspects of her Gloucestershire accent are compared, as is customary in English language study, with the regionally neutral accent called **Received Pronunciation** which has been referred to in chapters 1 and 3.

Exercise 2

Listen to the passage beginning *nineteen thirty-nine* and ending *I'm still going strong* (lines 3 to 9), and describe the differences between the Gloucestershire accent and of RP in terms of:
(a) rhythm and tempo, (b) pitch range and movement, (c) use of pauses, and (d) patterns of stress.

Commentary

Firstly, the tempo is extremely fast and the rhythm is staccato – almost like a machine-gun.

Secondly, the pitch of the voice is constrained within a narrow band of the speaker's range. Rather than her voice rising and falling like an RP speaker's might, she keeps it relatively high and level throughout the passage.

Thirdly, the passage has few 'natural breaks' within it. As explained in section 4.4 below, all speech is divided into blocks known as **tone-units**. Compared with the RP passages on the tape, Mrs Cook's speech is characterised by long, unbroken tone-units. The overall effect of the rhythmic and pitch features makes for a delivery reminiscent of an auctioneer calling for and repeating bids.

Finally, there is variation from RP in her placement of **primary stress** in words of more than one syllable. For example, her pronunciation of the word *advertisement* differs from the RP pronunciation *advertise-ment* – the third syllable, not the second, is stressed, with a consequent change in the pronunciation of the vowel.

(ii) Segmental features

Many of her vowels and consonants are different from an RP speaker's. One very obvious difference is in the stressed vowel in the words *paper* and *again*. As in RP, the sound is not a **single vowel** but a **diphthong** – the speaker glides from one vowel sound to another. The beginning part of the diphthong is similar to the one an RP speaker would use in the word *feet*, and the second part is similar to that in RP *cat*. Mrs Cook's pronunciation of *paper* and *again* might therefore be represented as *peeaper* and *ageean*. This pronunciation is restricted to a small area to the south-west of the Cotswold Hills. Some of the consonant features you will have noticed are characteristic of West Country speech more generally. One such feature is the /r/ sound in words like *cars*, *road-worke*r, and *thirty*. Even though we have the letter ⟨r⟩ in the spelling of these words, RP, together with most regional accents, does not have the /r/ in pronunciation. This is a comparatively recent development. Until the seventeenth century, all accents of English did pronounce the sound. Today only a few accents retain /r/ sounds before other consonants and at word endings. These accents, which include some of East Lancashire, much of Scots and the West Country, are called **rhotic** (*rho* is the Greek name for the letter ⟨r⟩).

Finally, there are two further related consonant features which distinguish West Country speech from that of other regions. These are the sounds we represent in writing by the letters ⟨s⟩ and ⟨f⟩. You will have noticed that in words such as *sweep*, *seed*, and *before*, the speaker replaces the sounds /s/ and /f/ with /z/ and /v/, *zweep*, *zeed*, *bevore*.

4.3   Boundaries of regional variation

Although we have been speaking of 'West Country English' as if it were a single, homogeneous variety, this is an idealisation of the facts. It has already been pointed out that Mrs Cook's pronunciation of *paper* is not common to the whole of the South-West.

Exercise

Listen to the second sample of West Country speech on tape. Mr Fred Archer also lives near the Cotswolds, in Ashton-under-Hill, which is to the north-east of Wotton-under-Edge. Identify those features of Mr Archer's pronunciation which are similar to, and those which are different from, Mrs Cook's.

```
he wore a (.) a thing like a pinafore smock made out of
sacking (.) with erm (.) some binder-twine round the
middle (.) and he got his battered old trilby (.) and he
used to keep his clay pipe stuck in his yorks when he
wasn't smoking it (.) and he smelt a mixture of Jeyes        5
Fluid (.) Stockholm tar (.) twist (.) tobacco (.) cider (.)
and erm (.) well and sheep I should say (.) not that he
wasn't clean mind you I mean he was a clean man but it was
just er (.) the (.) you know the (.) the smell of him (.)
and er (.) everything seemed to be erm (.) for a purpose    10
now he (.) had his thumb nails a bit on the long side
for getting the maggots out of the sheep you see (.) he er
grew them specially for that he never cut his thumb nails
very much (.) for maggoting the sheep you see . . .
that's right yes (.) and erm (.) then erm (.) he got        15
about three teeth at the front (.) which er (.) he used to
use for castrating the lambs and they came in very handy
```

(.) he drew the (.) he did the castration with his teeth
you see (.) and er (.) and then another spare time job of
his was doctoring cats he used to (.) put a pair of steel   20
spectacles on the (.) end of his nose and he looked real
professional when he was doing that . . .

Commentary

One consonant feature common to both speakers is the distribution of
/r/ sounds. Like Mrs Cook, Mr Archer produces /r/s at the ends of words
like *pinafore*, *ta*r, and *cide*r, and before other consonants in words like
purpose. However, if we turn our attention to /s/ and /f/, the two
speakers are obviously different.

In *pinafore* and *cider* we find Mr Archer using /f/ and /s/ rather than
/v/ and /z/. On the basis of recordings such as this, linguists have found
that the feature of rhoticity (sounding /r/ wherever it occurs in spelling)
extends much further North and East than does the tendency to replace
/f/ and /s/ with /v/ and /z/.

In describing the extent of any single accent feature, linguists use the
concept of **isophones**. An isophone is a line on a map which indicates
where one accent feature stops and another begins. Thus, on the map
opposite, the solid line is an isophone showing the extent of two different
pronunciations of the vowel in words like *cup* and *love*. The isophone
runs from the Bristol Channel on the West coast to the Wash on the
East coast. People living north of the line tend to pronounce *cup*,
love, *cut*, *mud* etc. with a vowel very similar to, or the same as RP *put*,
cushion, *butcher*. People south of the line would use a different vowel
in these words. They would therefore distinguish between pairs of
words like *put* and *putt*. For some Northern speakers, these words may
be **homophones** – words with different meanings but the same pronunciation.

The second, broken line on the map is the isophone relating to the
pronunciation of *grass*, *glass*, *path* etc. To the south of the line, the
vowel in these words is similar in quality to that used in *cart* and *jar*,
whereas to the north of the line it tends to be the same as that used in
cat, *pat*, and *mass*.

You will notice that although the two isophones do not follow
exactly the same line, they do approximately coincide. This, in fact,
reflects a general tendency for isophones to come in bundles or clusters;
where we find one isophone, very often there is another nearby.

North of the solid line, the vowel spelt ⟨u⟩ is pronounced by dialect speakers as /ʊ/, and south of the line as /ʌ/, e.g. /kʊp/v. /kʌp/, /lʊv/v. /lʌv/. North of the broken line, the vowel spelt ⟨a⟩ is pronounced by dialect speakers as /æ/, and south of the line as /ɑ/, e.g. /græs/ v. /grɑs/, /paeθ/ v. /paθ/

To return to the different pronunciations of /s/ – /z/ and /f/ – /v/ in the South-West, you will see from the second map below that the two isophones reflecting the north-eastern limits of the /z/ and /v/ also take broadly similar routes. There is a third isophone which follows the other two, though Mrs Cook's speech does not illustrate this. This is the pronunciation of ⟨th⟩ in words like *three* and *thumb*. People to the south-west of the line of the isophone tend to make no distinction between the ⟨th⟩ of *three* and *thumb* and that of *those* and *they*, both being pronounced with the ⟨th⟩ in RP *those* and *they*. People to the north-east of the line, however, do make the distinction found in RP.

Accent boundaries are not arbitrarily placed. Very often they correspond to other types of boundary such as natural geographical barriers, the past limits of trading circuits, and socio-political boundaries.

Before the development of motorised transport and other modern technology, natural boundaries like rivers and mountain ranges formed barriers to communication. As a result, the linguistic communities on each side of the boundary tended to develop in isolation from one another, each evolving its own distinctive pronunciation patterns, which have persisted into present-day English.

Market and trading patterns have also had a significant effect on the limits of accent variation. Until quite recently, rural villages conducted their agricultural trade almost exclusively through nearby centres of marketing and commerce. Even though two villages might be near to one another with no natural barrier between them, people from each village might seldom meet one another because they belonged to different trading circuits, and used different market towns. The isophones separating the speech represented by Mrs Cook from that represented by Mr Archer could partly be explained in these terms. Wotton-under-Edge fell within the sphere of influence of Bristol and the south-western market centres, whereas Ashton-under-Hill was within the trading circuit of the West Midlands towns.

Socio-political boundaries are also very important in determining the limits of accent features. For example, at the England-Scotland border in the North-West of England, there is no natural barrier that can explain the abrupt transition from English English to Scots English in the space of the few miles between Carlisle and Gretna Green. People living on opposite sides of socio-political boundaries may use different systems of speech to assert their different cultural identies. Accent is a means of aligning yourself with certain groups of people and of distinguishing yourself from other groups.

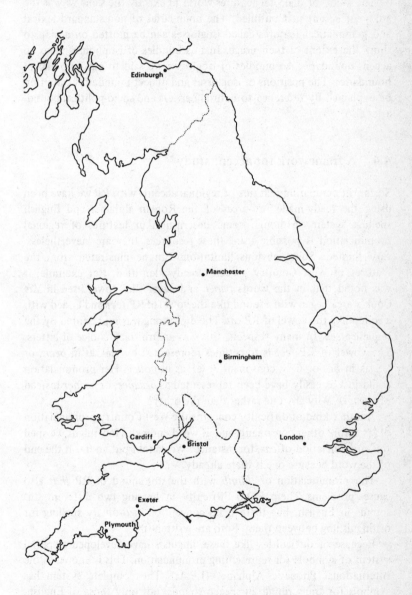

In the West Country area between the lines marked —·—·—, dialect speakers tend to pronounce the ⟨th⟩ of words like *thumb* as / ð /.

The study of dialectal features works in exactly the same way as the study of accent just outlined. The boundaries of non-standard lexical and grammatical features called **isoglosses** can be plotted on a map to show the extent of their usage. Just as bundles of isophones make up accent boundaries, so bundles of isoglosses are said to make up **dialect boundaries**. The positions of isoglosses and dialect boundaries can often be explained by reference to natural barriers and socio-political boundaries also.

4.4   A framework for accent study

So far, in comparing features of regional accents with RP we have been using the ready-made resources of the Roman alphabet and English spelling system. Although some description of features of regional pronunciation is possible using these resources, they are, nevertheless, very limited. Some obvious limitations can be illustrated from the features of West Country speech already identified. For example, it was noted that in the words *paper* and *again*, the vowel used in Mrs Cook's area began with a sound like the vowel of RP *feet* and ended with a sound like the vowel of RP *cat*. The diphthong was represented by the sequence *eea*. In many respects, this was an arbitrary choice of letters. The vowel of RP *feet* is sometimes represented by ⟨ea⟩, as in *bean*, or ⟨e⟩, as in *be*, or ⟨i⟩ + consonant + ⟨e⟩, as in *police*. Her pronunciation could just as easily have been represented as *peaaper*, or *peaper* instead of *peeaper*. Why any one rather than the other?

Another kind of difficulty concerns the West Country pronunciation of /r/ before other consonants and at word endings. How might we spell this pronunciation of *car*, for instance? We cannot put an ⟨r⟩ on the end of the word because one is there already.

The pronunciation of *thumb* with the ⟨th⟩ sound of RP *that* also causes problems. There is no difficulty in hearing two different ⟨th⟩ sounds in English, but there is no convention in ordinary spelling for distinguishing between them. Both are written ⟨th⟩.

Because of difficulties like these, linguists have developed a special system of symbols for representing pronunciation. This is known as the International Phonetic Alphabet (I.P.A.). The complete system has symbols for transcribing all speech sounds, not only those of English, together with a set of marks, or **diacritics**, which allow the transcriber to make subtle distinctions between sounds. For beginning purposes, however, many of the symbols and most of the diacritics can be ignored. You will be able to make significant progress using only a subset of 45 symbols.

Received Pronunciation is used as the reference accent, the one with which samples of regional speech are compared, so the selected symbols reflect the sound distinctions an RP speaker would make.

4.4.1 How to make a phonetic transcription
List of symbols to transcribe the segmental sounds of English
Simple vowels

i as in RP	bead	/bid/
ɪ	bid	/bɪd/
e	bed	/bed/
æ	bad	/bæd/
ɑ	bard	/bɑd/
ɒ	cod	/kɒd/
ɔ	board	/bɔd/
ʊ	put	/pʊt/
u	shoe	/ʃu/
ʌ	cup	/kʌp/
ɜ	bird	/bɜd/
ə	about, porter	/əbaʊt/, /pɔtə/

Diphthongs

eɪ	pay	/peɪ/
aɪ	pie	/paɪ/
ɔɪ	boy	/bɔɪ/
əʊ	go	/gəʊ/
aʊ	hound	/haʊnd/
ɪə	beer	/bɪə/
ɛə	bear	/bɛə/
ʊə	cure	/kjʊə/

Consonants

p	pit	/pɪt/
b	bit	/bɪt/
t	tip	/tɪp/
d	did	/dɪd/
k	kick	/kɪk/
g	give	/gɪv/
f	five	/faɪv/
v	vine	/vaɪn/

θ	thumb	/θʌm/
ð	this	/ðɪs/
s	some	/sʌm/
z	zoo	/zu/
ʃ	shoe	/ʃu/
ʒ	measure	/meʒə/
h	hot	/hɒt/
tʃ	charge	/tʃɑdʒ/
dʒ	gin	/dʒɪn/
m	mouse	/maʊs/
n	nice	/naɪs/
ŋ	sing	/sɪŋ/
l	leaf	/lif/
r	run	/rʌn/
j	yacht	/jɒt/
w	wet	/wet/
ʔ		occurs in some people's pronunciation of the medial consonant of words like *butter*, pronounced as *bu'er* (/bʌʔə/ or /bʊʔə/). See section 4.6.

There are two principles underlying this system of sound symbols:

(i)   Each symbol has a fixed and stable value, that is, it is used consistently to represent the same sound. For example, although in ordinary spelling the letter ⟨e⟩ sometimes represents the sound in *bet* and sometimes the sound in *be*, in phonetic transcription the sound /e/ always represents the vowel in *bet*.

(ii)   One symbol represents one segment in the 'speech chain', with only a very few exceptions. This is simpler than ordinary spelling, where a sequence of two or more letters may be used to represent one sound. For example, the vowel in *through* is represented by four letters, ⟨ough⟩, in spelling, but with one, /u/, in phonetic transcription.

The use of I.P.A. symbols provides a solution to the sorts of transcription problems already identified. In describing the pronunciation of *car*, for example, we write simply that an RP speaker says /kɑ/, and a West Country speaker says /kɑr/. Similarly, because the system has a symbol for both of the ⟨th⟩ consonants, we write that RP speakers say /θri/ and /ðæt/, and some West Country speakers say /ðri/ and /ðæt/.

Exercise

Listen to section 8 on the tape, where the sounds relating to the phonetic symbols are illustrated, with particular attention to the vowel sounds. Notice that there are 20 vowels in RP, and learn to distinguish them clearly.

4.5   Practical exercises in phonetic transcription

Exercise 1

Section 9 of the tape contains a passage spoken in RP. Listen to it and make a segmental transcription using phonetic symbols.

Commentary

In using phonetic symbols, you have transcribed the successive speech **segments** of the words. As mentioned in section 4.2, however, the **supra-segmental** features of pitch, loudness, rhythm, and tempo are also important elements of natural speech.

In the transcription printed below, the passage has been divided into sections known as **tone-units**. The boundaries of tone-units may be marked by a variety of features, including abrupt changes in pitch and/or loudness, short pauses, and lengthening of the last speech sound in the unit.

Within each tone-unit one syllable, called the **tonic** syllable, is more prominent than the others. This extra prominence is caused mainly by a definite movement of pitch over the syllable, which may continue over any following syllables within the tone-unit. Pitch movement can be rising, ╱ , falling, ╲ , rising-falling, ∧ , or falling-rising, ∨ . Different meanings and attitudes are conveyed by such pitch movements, called **tones**. In the transcription, tonic syllables are printed in bold type. Other syllables in tone-units carry stress also, but the tonic syllable, which usually specifies new information, stands out more.

Segmental and supra-segmental features may be transcribed separately or together. The following transcription of the passage in Exercise 1 uses ordinary spelling, and indicates the supra-segmental features only.

on the first day of British Su̯mmer Time | the winter
wea̱ther | has still got much of the coúntry | in its
gri̱p | with i̱cy roads | as far south as Ke̱nt | and
Hampshire | but it's still the No̯rth | that's mo̱st
affected | with the wo̱rst conditions | now moving   5
north-we̱stwards | into Sco̱tland |

Exercise 2

(a)   Using phonetic symbols, make a segmental transcription of the
section RP passage on the tape, section 10.

(b)   Divide the transcript into tone-units, underline the tonic syllables,
and mark in the tones above the tonic syllables, using the notation
given above.

You may find it difficult to agree on a common solution to supra-
segmental analysis in these exercises, especially in the placing and type
of the tonic syllable. More practice will be needed before you become
confident in any analysis of these features, if this is the first time you
have attempted one.

(N.B. an extended transcription of a dialogue, which includes the
identification of tone-units, tonic syllables and tones, is contained in
chapter 5, section 5.3. It may be helpful to refer to this.)

4.6   A practical exercise in describing a regional accent

Section 11 of the tape contains three samples of speech by two speakers
from the town of Ashington in Northumberland. A transcription of
each sample in ordinary spelling appears below.

Exercise 1

Listen to the Ashington speakers, following the speech from the transcriptions.

1.   even so (.) on Saturday nights (.) you'll probably remember the
street fights (.) I've often heard my wife er (.) tell me (.) that
that she's seen them out (.) standing in the street in their er

linings (.) sparring up and fighting (.) that was quite common on a Saturday night

2. times as far as I can remember when I was a young lad times was very very hard in Ashington (.) make no mistake about it (.) we were getting nothing (.) nothing (.) I'm only sixty seven year of age (.) and from about five year old till I was married until I started work we lived in dire poverty

3. we worked for nowt man (.) nothing (.) seven and fourpence a shift (.) I remember the first pay I got when I was married (.) I produced eighty ton of coal and I had thirty-nine bob (.) to take home to my wife (.) I'd ten bob rent to pay out of that

Exercise 2

Now compare the Northumberland accent with RP. Follow these instructions step by step to make a systematic description, beginning with the vowels:

(a) Identify the words which contain vowels pronounced /aʊ/ in RP, as in *about*, *out*, and write down the phonetic symbol for their Northumberland pronunciations.

(b) Repeat the exercise for the RP vowels /ɜ/, (*shirt*): /ɒ/, (*job*); /ɔ/, (*law*); /eɪ/, (*say*). You may find that an RP vowel has more than one pronunciation in Northumberland speech.

Exercise 3

Next, examine the consonants:

(a) Try to work out the pronunciations of /r/, which is particularly different from RP in the first extract.

(b) Identify the final consonant in words ending in ⟨-ing⟩ in their spelling.

(c) Note the pronunciation of ⟨t⟩ in the middle of a word.

Commentary

(i) The vowels

1. The vowel /aʊ/ in RP *about*, *out*, tends to be pronounced /u/.

The relationship between RP and Northumberland pronunciation can be set down as follows:

RP	Northumberland	Evidence
/aʊ/ ——▶	/u/	*out* (extract 2), *about* (extract 3)

where the arrow ——▶ means 'tendency to replace one sound with the other'.

2.   The relationship between the other vowels is:

/ ɜ / ——▶	/ ɔ /	*worked, thirty, first*
/ ɒ / ——▶	/ ə /	*bob*
/ ɔ / ——▶	/aʊ/	*fourpence*

3.   The vowel /eɪ/ has more than one **realisation**. In the word *pay* (extract 2), it is like a long RP /ɪ/ sound. This is the most usual realisation for this accent, and can be represented by placing a colon after the /ɪ/ symbol to denote lengthening, /ɪ:/.

A second realisation is found in the word *eighty* in the same sample. Here the vowel is very similar to the RP *buy*, /aɪ/. This replacement with /aɪ/ occurs only in the word *eight* and its compounds *eighteen* and *eighty*.

The third realisation is found a few words later in *take*, where the vowel is pronounced /eɪ/. This pronunciation is also highly restricted and occurs in two words only, the other being *make*.

/eɪ/ ——▶	* /ɪ:/	*pay*
	/aɪ/	*eighty*
	/e/	*take*

* = the standard form for the Northumberland accent.

(ii)   The consonants

The first prominent consonant feature is the pronunciation of /r/. The difference between the Northumberland and RP /r/ is most noticeable in extract 1, *remember* and *probably*. It is similar to the /r/ of French and German. Instead of being produced with the tongue behind the tooth ridge at the front of the mouth, it is made with the back of the tongue against the uvula (the small 'finger' of fleshy tissue that hangs down from the very back of the palate). The symbol for this, not included in the list of sounds, is /ʀ/.

Another common consonant feature in Northumberland, but not restricted to it, is the replacement of /ŋ/ with /n/ at word endings. This is most noticeable in extract 1, in *linings* (a dialect word for men's combination underwear) and *sparring*.

A third consonant difference is in the realisation of /t/. The word *Saturday* in extract 1 does not have the sort of /t/ that occurs in RP *top*. Some people might say that there is no consonant at the end of the first syllable, and a novelist might substitute an apostrophe for the ⟨t⟩ and write the word as *Sa'urday* (cf. chapter 9 on dialect in literature). In phonetic terms, however, there is a consonant there, produced within the larynx (behind the 'Adam's apple'). It has the technical name **glottal stop**, and is symbolised as /ʔ/. It occurs in many accents, and is often referred to as 'sloppy pronunciation' when used in words like *better* and *butter*.

/r/	⟶	/R/	*probably*, *remember*, *street*
/t/	⟶	/ʔ/	*Saturday*
/ŋ/	⟶	/n/	*linings*, *sparring*

Exercise 4

Listen to the two samples of the London accent on the tape, sections 12 and 13.
(a) Transcribe the speech.
(b) Identify the differences in vowel and consonant pronunciation between the London accent and RP, and describe them in the way which has been demonstrated.

4.7   Social evaluation of accents

On the whole, regional accents tend to be stigmatised together with the words and grammar of their dialect. The description of accents is often pejorative, that is, they are disparaged and not valued highly. The claims made against the use of regional accents fall into three main types:

(a) they are simply incorrect ways of speaking,
(b) they are ugly, and lack aesthetic appeal,
(c) they are lazy and imprecise.

Exercise

(a)   Question informants about their opinions on regional accents.
(This topic could be added to the questions in the Acceptability
Test in chapter 1, or form the subject of a separate investigation.)

(b)   Discuss the opinions that you discover, and say whether there is
any relationship between the social class of the persons interviewed and their attitudes towards regional accents.

(c)   Discuss the validity of these views on regional accents.

Commentary

(i)   The 'incorrectness' view

This raises the main topic of chapter 1 again. Just as there is a strong
tendency for people to look upon the regionally neutral system of
Standard English as the correct one, and then to use it as a 'measuring
rod' for evaluating regional dialects, so the regionally neutral accent,
RP, is used to measure regional accents.

To what extent is RP the correct way of speaking? If people agree
that one form of behaviour is the correct form, then that behaviour
becomes the standard by which others are judged. However, it is important to remember that such standards are matters of fashion and
convention.

For example, at one time all accents of English were rhotic. The
sound /r/ was pronounced before consonants and at the end of words
by everyone. However, in the seventeenth century it became fashion-
able in Court circles to drop the pronunciation of /r/ except where it
occurred before vowels. The accent associated with the Court had social
prestige, and developed later into present-day RP. The dropping of /r/
spread to other regional accents. Today the pronunciation of *car* and
part as /kɑ/ and /pɑt/ is generally more socially acceptable than the
West Country older pronunciation /kɑr/ and /pɑrt/.

But in the United States, the situation is reversed. The pronunciation with /r/ present has more prestige, and the non-rhotic accents
have low status and are called 'incorrect'.

RP, therefore, cannot be the correct pronunciation in any absolute
sense. What counts as correct is simply a matter of social convention,
relative to time and place.

(ii) The 'ugliness' view

You may hear people talking about Northern accents as 'flat', or Glasgow vowels as 'harsh', or saying that the Birmingham accent is 'not melodious'. When speakers of British English are presented with samples of accents and asked to rate them on a scale according to how pleasant they sound, they broadly agree that RP should come near the top, together with certain South-Eastern accents. Highland Scots and West Country are usually rated highly too.

Accents from Newcastle, Liverpool, Glasgow, and Birmingham, however, are rated negatively. These ratings are often justified on the grounds of ugliness, harshness, and so on, but it can be no coincidence that the accents which receive the poorest ratings are all from industrial cities. It seems that people are reacting to the social connotations of the areas from which the accents come.

This is confirmed by the reactions of speakers who are unfamiliar with the social connotations of the accents about which they are asked to make aesthetic judgements. They often rate the accents of the big industrial cities more highly than those of RP and the rural South and South West.

(iii) The 'impreciseness' view

The words *lazy* and *sloppy* are often used to express this negative view of regional accents. The glottal stop replacement of /t/ is frequently cited as an example. But if you examine accents which have glottal stop replacement, it becomes clear that the use of /ʔ/ is by no means sloppy or haphazard. Not all /t/s can be replaced by /ʔ/. The possibility of replacement is governed by the position of /t/ within a word. No accent of British English allows /t/ at the beginning of a word (word initial) to be pronounced as /ʔ/. The word *top* is never pronounced / ʔop/. The possibility of replacement can only apply to /t/s which are in the middle of words (word medial), or at the end (word final). Thus we find pronunciations such as /beʔə/ for *better*, and /beʔ/ for *bet* in a number of accents. Far from being sloppy, the use of the glottal stop is an orderly business, governed by linguistic rules concerning the position of /t/.

Another aspect of the 'impreciseness' argument suggests that children with regional accents may have difficulties in learning to read and write. One well-aired example concerns the dropping of /h/, which is characteristic of London, Yorkshire, and Lancashire accents, and others. Children who drop their /h/s, the argument goes, will have difficulty in distinguishing between pairs of words such as *hill* and *ill* in writing.

However, *all* accents, including RP, contain many pairs of words that are homophones. Is there not equal difficulty in distinguishing *hour* from *our*? Consider also the tendency in RP to pronounce *tower* and *tar* as homophones, /tɑ/.

A measured, linguistic consideration of people's negative reactions to regional speech leads again and again to the view that, no matter what other reasons are put forward in explanation, the issue is really one of social prejudice. An objective study of accent can help to modify the instant reaction that we all tend to have towards an accent which is marked as socially inferior.

4.8 Accents and social variables

Accents vary not only geographically, but according to certain social variables, that is, accents are associated with different social groups.

The first, and most obvious, social grouping related to accent is social class. Although we often label regional accents as coming from particular geographical areas – a city or a county for example – it is clear that not everyone in that area will speak in the same way. Social class seems to stand in *inverse* relationship to regional accent. That is, the higher up the social and occupational ladder we look, the fewer regional features we find. Thus, although people in professional jobs from different areas of the country may have some pronunciation features which are regional, the differences between them are less marked than for unskilled manual workers.

The second and less obvious feature is gender, or the differences between women's and men's speech. Recent research has shown that within any social class, men show a greater tendency than women to use the 'broadest', most regionally marked, pronunciation. The reasons for this are not yet clear, but one possibility is that teachers and parents may tend to correct girls' speech more than boys'.

When you have studied this chapter, you should be much more aware of the differences in pronunciation that you hear, and able to say more precisely which features are the most marked, in terms of vowels and consonants, pitch and intonation. Your opinions on the controversial aspects of attitudes towards dialect and accent may have changed, but these remain your own, and you must question everything that has been said here, except the objective linguistic facts.

Exercise

Read again the extracts from Peter Trudgill's and John Honey's books at the end of chapter 1, and apply the arguments specifically to regional and social accents.

Discuss the debate between the view that would stress the linguistic validity of all accents, and the view that the social consequences of speaking a marked regional accent must be a first consideration.

5

Spoken English and written English

5.1 Speech and writing as media for language

We all learn to talk before we learn to read and write. Chapter 6 describes in more detail how children learn to talk. This chapter discusses the principal differences between **speech** and **writing** as media for language. That is, we assume that the same **language**, English, underlies talking and writing, listening and reading. Language in this sense is abstract, something we know. When we use it, it must be made concrete, and transmitted and received by one or more of the human senses.

Consider the alternative realisation of language which is available to the deaf, **signing**. Like writing, sign language is read with the eye, but uses the human body itself to signify the words. And what is available to those who are both deaf and blind? Communication through the sense of touch alone is possible, as the life of Helen Keller made clear.

Speech consists of sounds, and writing of marks on a surface, and this fundamental difference produces equally marked contrasts in our use of the two media. Some of the differences are the result of the fact that we listen to speech, which is impermanent (unless tape-recorded), and usually we can see who is talking to us. Hence there is always the possibility of **feedback** between speaker and listener. The telephone is a special case, and produces its own characteristic features of **discourse**. We must read writing. It is permanent and can be reread. We do not usually see the writer, so communication is one way only. There is no feedback during the interchange.

These differences of **substance** (sound or marks on a surface), and of **function** (what we can do with spoken or written language), result in differences of **form** and **style**. Rather than list these differences, we shall look closely at some authentic speech and writing, and help you to discover for yourself what these examples show.

Transcribing speech into writing freezes it in a form which we can study. If speech can be turned into writing, and writing can be read aloud, you may wonder whether there can be any essential differences. There are, as you will find out.

5.2   Making a transcription

In transcribing speech into writing you have the choices of method discussed in chapter 4: ordinary or phonetic spelling, with or without an indication of certain supra-segmental features. Your choice will depend upon the purpose for which you are making the transcription.

For the dialogue in section 5.3, ordinary spelling, or **orthography** is used, as the chapter focuses on aspects of speech in which segmental features of pronunciation are not important. Because **intonation** and **stress** are closely bound up with meaning and information in speech, supra-segmental (or **prosodic**) features are shown.

Pauses are also significant in speech. In conjunction with different tones, they have a grammatical function similar to that of punctuation in writing, but they also have additional functions in discourse between speakers (see chapter 6). A momentary break or micropause is shown as (.) and a longer pause is shown as a figure in seconds, e.g. (2.0). These pauses are silent; others are 'filled' with *er* or *um* and similar sounds. A pause which includes an intake of breath is marked (.h).

Unfinished words are marked with a full stop. Where there is an overlap between the speakers, the place where the overlap begins is marked // in the transcription of the first speaker.

Features which break the flow of speech are quite usual and necessary. Remember that when you speak spontaneously you are doing at least three things at once: planning what to say next, saying what you have planned, and monitoring what you are saying in order to check that it is what you meant to say. It is, therefore, not surprising that ordinary spontaneous speech in conversation is broken up by hesitations, false starts, self-corrections, repetitions, fillers, and so on. They have been referred to as **normal non-fluency features** of speech. They are not part of the vocabulary or grammar of language, and by definition cannot be a feature of a written document (except in rough drafts with alterations, which we don't usually let others read).

In the following transcription, the non-fluency features are printed in italics, leaving an 'edited text'.

(N.B. The commentary in section 5.3 is deliberately restricted to a discussion of ways in which speech contrasts with writing in its structure. Other important aspects of spoken language which are related to the functions of intonation, pitch, and stress, are not discussed. The transcription of supra-segmental features is included for the benefit of teachers and lecturers who wish to use the data to explore these other functions.)

5.3 Dialogue 1: Making a model village

A nine-year-old girl called Romy had a conversation with her father, which was tape-recorded. She had been amusing herself in the holidays by making a model village market, after watching a Blue Peter programme on television. Her father got her to talk about it and then asked her to write down what she had been telling him about the market she had made.

Notice that he asks questions, partly to start the dialogue and to keep it going, and partly because he wants to question things she hasn't made clear. Some parts of their talk will show features that belong to **discourse**, or **verbal interaction**. One will complete another's utterance, for example. Certain words, like *Well* . . ., when starting a sentence, have a discourse function.

Exercise 1

Transcribe the first minute of the conversation before looking at the transcription printed below, making sure that you include everything you hear.

Exercise 2

Then listen to the whole conversation, following it with the transcription.

Exercise 3

Make a list of the ways in which Romy's use of English in speech differs from her use of the language in writing.

One important clue to the difference can be presented in the first place as a question: can you divide Romy's speech into **sentences**? Do grammatical units and tone-units coincide?

5.3.1 Transcription of the spoken dialogue (Cassette tape Section 14)

F. so what have you been making Ro?|

R. *(.h)* (3.0) well *I was ma. I've been making a mar.* I've been making a market| *(.h)* (3.0) and I made it out of matchsticks| and (1.0) *(.h)* em matchboxes| *(.h) and* (.) at the bottom of the matchboxes| *I I put (.h)* I put matches| (.) *for* for four legs| 5
(1.0) and then *(.h)* I put four matches at the top| *(.h)* and I put a roof at the top| (1.0) *em* out of paper| *(.h)* and then I made little things to put on it| *(.h) er*

F. you've been making what?| a market?|

R. yeah| 10

F. *so* and you've been using *match.(.)* matchboxes?|

R. and matchsticks|

F. what did you use the box part for?|
(1.0)

R. that was for the table| 15

F. oh I see| (.) the stall was it?|

R. yeah| *(.h) and* (.) and then I made lots of those· *(.h)* (3.0) and later on I'm going to (.) finish it off by making a village square| *(.h) and I make the village square by* (3.0) *(.h) well I'm going to put* I'm going to put *er (.h) benches for* (.) benches| and I'm   20
going to put bins around the place| and bus-stops| *(.h)* and I'm going to put my market on| *(.h)* (3.0) *em*

F. have you made any things to go on the stalls?|
(1.0)

R. yes *I made f. (.h)* I've made fruit| and (1.0) *(.h)* (bread| and (.)   25
flowers| *and* (.)

F. what did you use to make all those things?|

R. *(.h)* well for my fruit| and the bread| *em* I used plasticine| *(.h)* and (.) for my flowers I used crepe paper|
(2.0)   30

F. so how did you make (1.0) the fruit (.) with the plasticine?|

R. I just came to put them in the shape of the fruit|
(3.0)

F. what rolled them *or s.*?|

R. well it depends what kind of a **shape** really| if they're bananas 35
I made them in a long line and **curved** them| *(.h)* and if they were
apples I made them into a **ball**|*(.h)* and I had (.) pears what *I* (.)
I had quite a **trouble** making those|*(.h)*

F. why's **that**?|

R. because I couldn't quite get it the quite **shape**| *it* it was **poin-** 40
ted at the top| when it went round| *(.h)* and it went into a great
big **ball**| *(.h)* it looked a bit funny so I had to try and get it so it
was kind of **sloped** into a ball|

F. oh I **see**| (.) did you have *er* (.) *have* to **paint** them?|

R. *(.h)* yeah I painted them **black**| (1.0) **oh**| (1.0) I painted the 45
stalls black|
(1.0)

F. oh I **see**| (.) but I meant the **fruit**| (.) did you // (1.0) have to

R.   no

F. **paint** them?| 50

R. no because *they had the c.* the plasticine was **coloured**|

F. ah I **see**| (.) so what colours did you use for **what**?|

R. *(.h)* well for the apples I used **green**| *(.h)* (2.0) and for (.) bananas
I used **yellow**|*(.h) for the* (3.0) **no**| for the apples I used **red**|
(2.0) and for the *(.h)* pears I used **green**| (3.0) *er* (1.0) *and I* 55
(1.0) that's all I could really **make** those kind of fruits| but
I made (1.0) about **two** of each kind|*(.h)* (2.0) *and* (.) and I
used **brown** for my bread rolls| and just*(.h)* put them into a kind of
(3.0) *em* a **rectangle**|

F. **rectangular** shape?| 60

R. yeah *(.h)* and put a **line** at the top| to make it more like **bread**|
because (.h) sometimes they put lines in the **middle**|

F. when they're **baking** them?|

R. yeah // *(.h)* (2.0) *em*

F.   mm   65

F. you said you made **flowers** didn't you?|

R. yes I just screwed up some (1.0) crepe **paper**| *it* (.) and it (.) *it*
did look a bit like *em* **flowers**|

F. were they in **bunches**?|
(2.0)   70

R. no I just put (1.0) *I just put* lines of (.) screwed up **paper**|

F. but they look // (1.0) quite like **flowers**|

R.   *yeah they look*

R. yeah

F. and they were all different colours as well?| 75
R. yeah
F. so you've got bread| (1.0) flowers| (1.0) fruit| (1.0) what else?|
(1.0)
R. well| (3.0) *well (.h)* I had a material stall| *(.h)* and for that I
got matchsticks again| *(.h) and got* and got little bits of (.) 80
material| and rolled them round| and then put them on the stall|
F. oh that was a good idea| (.) was that your idea?|
(3.0)
R. well (.) I got it while *(.h)* I was watching Blue Peter| that's how I
got the idea| 85
F. for everything?|
(2.0)
R. *(.h)* no| (.) well *(.h) they made* they made the stalls a bit different
to me| *(.h)* and *they just* they didn't make a village| // (.) they
F.   mm 90
R. just (.) made these stalls|
F. but what about the (2.0) *the* material rolls| did
R. oh yes that // bit|
F.   that was their idea?|
R. yeah 95
F. yeah
R. they didn't use plasticine for the *(.h)* bread rolls| they (.) they
made it out of special baking stuff| (.) *stuff* what won't go mouldy
though| (1.0) they made real *br.* | (1.0) *real* (.) things *(.h)* I've
forgotten what they used for the fruit though| 100
(3.0)
F. o.k.| well that sounds (.) as if you've been having a good time| (.)
can I go and have a look at it now?|
R. yes|

5.3.2 Romy's writing

The market I made

These are the things I used. I used dead matches and
match box's and plasticene. First I stuck the matches at
the bottom of the match box's for legs. Then I stuck four
at the top of the match box and then made a roof out of
paper. Later on I painted it black. When it had dried I 5
made the things to go on them. I made fruit, bread,

flowers, then I made a material shop by rolling material
round matches. I made the bread and fruit with
plasticene. The flowers were made out of screwed up crate
paper. Then I'm going to make a villige to put the   10
stalls on.

Commentary

Her written version is much shorter than the conversation. She omits
quite a lot of the information she talked about, and she also puts some
of it in a different order. This is to be expected from a nine-year-old.
Writing takes more thought and effort than talking. But she has written
enough for us to notice some important differences. Look first at the
structure, or how the bits of information are linked and related.

In her writing, Romy correctly places a capital letter at the beginning, and a full-stop at the end of her sentences (except, perhaps,
sentence 7?). Setting out a text in columns is often helpful in sorting
out its sentence structure. If a sentence consists of more than one
clause, each clause is put on a separate line. Words which have a linking
function are separated from the main part of the clause, as follows:

Linking words		*Clauses*
1.		These are the things I used.
2.		I used dead matches and match box's
		and plasticene.
3.	First	I stuck the matches at the bottom
		of the match box's for legs.
4a.	Then	I stuck four at the top of the
		match box
4b.	and then	Ø made a roof out of paper.
5.	Later on	I painted it black.
6a.	When	it had dried
6b.		I made the things to go on them.
7a.		I made fruit, bread, flowers,
7b.	then	I made a material shop,
7c.	by	rolling material around matches.
8.		I made the bread and the fruit with
		plasticene.
9.		The flowers were made out of
		screwed up crate paper.

10a. Then   I'm going to make a villige
10b.   to put the stalls on.

If her spoken response to her father's first question is printed it as if it were written language, it looks like this:

I've been making a market **and** I made it out of matchsticks and matchboxes **and** at the bottom of the matchboxes I put matches for four legs **and** then I put four matches at the top **and** I put a roof out of paper **and** then I made little things to put on it.

It is fully **grammatical**, but not **acceptable** as good written English because it consists of a series of clauses all joined, or **coordinated**, by *and*. Compare the linking words in her writing. What is normal and goes unnoticed in speech would look wrong in writing. It is a matter of convention, so she changed her spoken English to conform to an acceptable style in her writing, though without really knowing how.

The question in Exercise 3 asked what a sentence is in speech. There are no capital letters or full stops to tell us. In Romy's first utterance there are six **main clauses**. Is it one sentence just because she happened to pause at that point? Suppose she had gone on uninterrupted with *and... and then... and then...?*

Can we define a sentence? Here, for example, is a confident definition from a Victorian grammar book called *The Analysis of Sentences* (1859):

Language is the utterance of our thoughts in words. The complete utterance of a single thought is called *A Sentence*.

Exercise 4

Discuss this definition of a sentence, apply it to Romy's talk, and to her writing. Is it a satisfactory definition?

Commentary

(i) The functions of the word and
In her opening utterance, Romy uses *and* five times to join her clauses.

In her writing, she uses *and* only once for this purpose. Her other uses of *and* are for joining **phrases** and **words**. She avoids the normal spoken use of *and* as a kind of all-purpose linker, or **continuer**.

Listen to the tape-recording again, and notice how she uses intonation, stress, and pauses like spoken punctuation, to divide up her speech into manageable units of information. The function of written punctuation marks is partly equivalent to some of the functions of intonation, stress, and pauses. That is why we can read aloud from a written text. But it will always sound like reading aloud, and not like spontaneous speech.

In a similar way in reverse, we have seen that speech doesn't look like authentic writing when transcribed.

So the **coordinating conjunction** *and* has two uses in speech. Firstly as a grammatical word, joining sentences, clauses, phrases and words, just as in writing. Secondly, and only in spoken English, as a linking word or continuer between groups of clauses (or **clause-complexes**) where its function is not just grammatical, but also part of conversational exchange, telling a listener, 'Don't interrupt, I haven't finished.'

(ii) Deletion

If *and* joins two clauses, and the second clause has the same grammatical subject as the first, the second subject may be **deleted**.

For example, Romy's written sentence (4) omits *I* in the second clause (4b) – 'and then ∅ made a roof out of paper' (the sign ∅ is used to mark a deleted item). When you find examples of deletion, or **ellipsis**, you have direct evidence of *and* as a grammatical conjunction.

Exercise 5

The writing has 15 clauses, but *and* is used only once to coordinate clauses. Her talk has 66 clauses (not counting *yes* and *no* and other very short responses), and 25 uses of *and* between clauses. The difference is very marked.

Examine the uses of *and* in Romy's talk, and divide them into the two categories.

Exercise 6

Write out Romy's spoken narrative in clauses.

Here is part of it as an example:

Father	Romy
how did you make the fruit with the plasticene?	I just came to put them in the shape of the fruit
what rolled them?	well it depends what kind of a shape really
	if they were bananas
	I made them in a long line
	and Ø curved them
	and if they were apples
	I made them into a ball
	and I had pears
	what I had quite a trouble
	making those

To sum up so far, spoken English tends to be marked by features of non-fluency which are often only apparent when speech is transcribed and read, because they are a normal part of our way of talking.

Particularly when telling a story, we link our spoken clauses together with *and* so that the boundaries of sentences may be impossible to determine. This is not so in writing, because we learn not to use *and* like this, and punctuation clearly marks the beginning and end of sentences. In this way, the style of spoken English is usually in marked contrast to that of written English.

The grammatical structure of speech is often less complex than that of writing. This is not very noticeable in Romy's speech and writing, because at nine years old she has not yet acquired the skills of complex writing, but you can see it more clearly in the following transcription and text, spoken and written by her older sister.

These stylistic features of spoken and written English are, of course, always associated with the context in which we use either medium. As a result, we say that spoken English is more **informal** than written English, because we usually use writing for purposes that are **formal** (although there are many occasions when we speak formally and write informally, of course).

Using a tape-recording of a conversation, we are in fact eavesdropping on people we don't know. We cannot see them, and so have to guess at their gestures and facial expressions (called **paralinguistic** features), and the kind of place in which they were talking (the **context of situation**).

It is possible that some references made by the speakers cannot be properly understood, and so remain inexplicit, because language is only a part of how we communicate meaning.

Exercise 7

Examine the transcription and listen again to the tape to find:
(a) some examples of inexplicitness of language, and
(b) supply some of the probable paralinguistic gestures and visible signs used by the speakers.

5.4 Dialogue 2: At the riding school

Romy's elder sister Rebecca, who was 12 years old, was recorded in a similar conversation and then wrote about her experiences at riding school. Here first is the unedited text of her writing, followed by an unedited and unmarked transcription of the opening part of her talk.

5.4.1 Rebecca's writing

When you go to a riding school everything apart from riding the horse will be done for you. However if you have a horse of your own you have to do everything yourself.

Before you mount (get on) a horse it has to have a saddle and bridle put on it, this is called 'tacking up'.   5

When saddling a horse you need a saddle and a girth. A girth is a long strap which, when the saddle has been put on the horse's back, is buckled to one side and is then brought under his stomach and buckled tightly to the other   10 side of the saddle. This stops the saddle from falling off.

Lift the saddle high above the horse's back and then bring down gently so that the front (pommel) of the saddle is over the horse's withers. Slide the saddle down onto   15 the horse's back until it fits snugly. The sliding down of the saddle is done so that the hairs on the horse's back all lie down the right way. Looking from the back of

the horse you should be able to see a channel of light
between the lining of the saddle. You should also be able   20
to slide your hand under the pommel of the saddle, this is
so that air can get to the horse's back.

The first thing you will learn, when having your first
riding lesson, is to mount correctly.

Face the horse's tail, hold the reins in your left hand   25
and rest this hand on the pommel of the saddle. Turn the
stirrup iron towards you.

Slip your left foot into the stirrup iron. Turn round
so you are facing the horse's side then spring up. Swing
your right leg over the saddle then lower yourself gently   30
into the saddle.

There is a special position when riding. This position
in no way should appear stiff. Your back should be
straight, yet relaxed, your arms should hang from the
shoulders, with your elbows bent and slightly touching   35
your sides of your body. Your hands should be 6" apart
and must keep a 'feel' of the horse's mouth. The ball of
the foot should be on the stirrup iron, the heel pushed
down and the toes in a natural position.

The paces   40
A walk is slow pace and easy to master, but the trot is
more difficult. The trot is a bumpy pace and to make it
comfortable to ride, the rider rises for one bump and sits
down in the saddle for another.

To make a horse canter you make him go into a trot by   45
increasing your leg pressure on his side. But instead of
rising for one bump and sitting down in the saddle for
another you sit down in the saddle all the time. If you
wish to make the horse canter in a circle his inside leg
must go farther than the outside one. To make the inside   50
leg go farther you put your inside leg on the girth and
your outside leg behind the girth. Then increase your leg
pressure against his sides and he should go into a canter,
if he does not use your stick against his side.

To make your horse jump you must ride him on towards the   55
jump, if he runs out to the left pull his right rein and
kick him with your left leg and vice versa. When taking
off and going over the jump your horse will stretch out

his neck, lean forward and give him lots of rein so you do
not restrict his head.   60

5.4.2 Transcription of part of the dialogue (Cassette tape Section 15)

F. o.k. Reb (.) are you going to tell me something about riding?
   (2.0)
R. yeah what do you want to know?
   (2.0)
F. (.h) well (.) when you go riding (.) to the riding school (.) what's 5
   involved?
R. well first we just mount (2.0) and w.(.) we mount by going to the
   left side or the near side of the pony (.) and we put our left foot
   in the stirrup (1.0) and then we sort of jump round until we're
   facing the pony's side (1.0) and then (.) and then we jump up (.) 10
   and then we swing our right (.) leg over and then go gently down to
   the saddle so we don't give the horse a fright if we went (.h) bump
   down
F. oh so the horses are all (1.0) s. they've got the saddles on before
   you start then   15
   (2.0)
R. yeah // yeah
F.   the bridles (.) you don't have to do anything about them
R. no (1.0) (.h) but (.h) but when we went on the Boxing Day ride
   we had to do that   20
F. put the saddles on?
R. yeah (.h) and (1.0) what you do is you get the saddle and a girth
   which you tie round the pony's tummy well (.h) it's sort of like a
   strap (.) with buckles on the end (.h) and you get this saddle (.h)
   you put (.) lift it quite high above the pony's head but not really 25
   really high (1.0) well not the head but back (.h) and then you lower
   it down on to his withers which is just above his back and slide it
   down (.h) and if you didn't slide it th. the hairs would all b. (.)
   be all the wrong way (.h) and it'd hurt the pony because it'd rub
   against the saddle (1.0) (.h) and then you've got to get the   30
   stirrups and (1.0) I mean the (.h) the girth (1.0) and buckle it to
   one side and bring it under the (.) pony's tummy (2.0) (.h) and then
   buckle it to the other side and (.h) often when you do that they
   blow their tummy out so that when they're on a ride they (.h) they
   can (1.0) bring the tummy back in (1.0) and it'll be quite   35
   comfortable (.h) but but most people (.) kick them in the tummy
   and then they go (1.0) thin [the conversation continues]

Exercise 1

Transcribe the remainder of the dialogue.

Exercise 2

Collect examples of normal non-fluency features from the transcription, and classify them as hesitations, false starts, self-corrections, or fillers.

   You will find that these categories overlap, so don't expect each example to fall neatly into one set or the other.

Exercise 3

Take a 'paragraph' of Rebecca's talk and turn it into good written style. Then describe what you have done to the original to achieve this.

Exercise 4

Is Rebecca's talk similar to Romy's in the frequency of the conjunction *and*?

   Are the sentence boundaries of Rebecca's talk as clear as those of her writing?

Exercise 5

Is the sentence structure of her writing simpler or more complex than that of her speech? Quote examples when commenting.

Exercise 6

Examine the interaction between Rebecca and her father for features which show that they are in a face-to-face situation, using gesture as well as speech, aware of each other and reacting to each other.

   Give examples from the language used which give you the information.

Exercise 7

Make a comparison between the following extract from her talk and the corresponding section of her writing. Look especially for features of

vocabulary and grammar that you would describe as **formal** or **informal**.
Which of these categories best fits the speech and the writing?

Saddling up
  spoken:

	what you do is	
	you get the saddle and a girth	
	which you tie around the pony's tummy	
well	it's sort of like a strap with buckles on the end	
and	you get this saddle	5
	you lift it quite high above the pony's head	
but	not really really high	
well	not the head but back	
and then	you lower it down on to his withers which is just	
	above his back	10
and	Ø slide it down	
and if	you didn't slide it	
	the hairs would be all the wrong way	
and	it'd hurt the pony	
because	it'd rub against the saddle	15
and then	you've got to get the girth	
and	Ø Ø Ø buckle it to one side	
and	Ø Ø Ø bring it under the pony's tummy	
and then	Ø Ø Ø buckle it to the other side	

  written:

When	saddling a horse	
	you need a saddle and a girth.	
	A girth is a long strap	
	which . . is buckled to one side	
when	the saddle has been put on the horse's back	5
and	Ø is then brought under his stomach,	
and	Ø Ø buckled tightly to the other side of the saddle.	
	This stops the saddle from falling off.	
	Lift the saddle high above the horse's back	
and	then bring down gently	10
so that	the front (pommel) of the saddle is over	
	the horse's withers.	
	Slide the saddle down onto the horse's back	
until	it fits snugly.	

| | The sliding down of the saddle is done | 15 |
| so that | the hairs on the horse's back all lie down the right way. | |

Exercise 8

Select another pair of parallel extracts from Rebecca's speech and writing, and discuss their differences and similarities.

Exercise 9

Use part of the conversation to identify some of the prosodic (suprasegmental) features of Rebecca's speech:

(a)   intonation: mark some tonic syllables and the tone, or direction of pitch movement on them;
(b)   stress: find words which Rebecca speaks with contrastive stress, or emphasis;
(c)   tempo, loudness, and rhythm: find examples of her delivery which are faster or slower, louder or softer than the norm, or which show marked changes of rhythm.

In all these examples that you discover, relate the prosodic features to her meaning, or to the effect that she wishes to produce.

6

Learning to talk

6.1 Language learning a complex skill

If you have had the experience of learning a foreign language, you will have some idea of the range of knowledge which is needed in properly speaking, reading and writing that language. You have to learn about pronunciation, spelling, words and their meanings, and how to construct sentences with the words in the right order. Then there are different ways of constructing messages so as to be interesting, logical, persuasive, tactful, polite and so on.

The way we learn a second language after we have already learned our first will differ from the way we learned the first one, because knowledge of our first language is bound to affect our learning of the new language, in helpful and unhelpful ways. Nevertheless, attempting to learn a new language can highlight the nature and complexity of the skills involved in knowing a language.

If we consider just what goes on when children learn their first language, we can begin to appreciate the true nature and complexity of the skills which they have. All normal children learn to talk surprisingly quickly, and most of them, by the age of four, can talk on a wide variety of topics, using language that is clearly spoken, rich in vocabulary, varied in the patterns of sentence used, subtle in shades of meaning expressed, and appropriate to the situation and purpose.

We shall try to show more exactly what a four-year-old's skills in language use are by looking at successive stages in the development of speech. Argument still goes on about how a child can learn so effortlessly the complex skills that using language involves. After four years of learning a foreign language in school, when you were not a young child, could you speak it as fluently as your first language?

These attempts to explain how children acquire their first language have been set out as **hypotheses**, that is, principled guesses. They depend to some extent upon ideas about what language itself is, and research over the last twenty years or so has come up with three main hypotheses:

1. Children learn language by **imitating** the people they hear talk to them - usually their parents and family.
2. Children learn language because they are **programmed** to do so, just as a bird is programmed to build a nest or to migrate. This is not to say that a French child is programmed to learn French and a Chinese child to learn Chinese, but that all children are programmed to learn any language they are exposed to in infancy, because all languages have certain **universal features**. Children, in this hypothesis, are supposed to have special mental capacities which are designed to make the task of language learning possible.
3. Children learn language because they are very clever when compared with animals like chimpanzees, for example. Their intelligence is not so much different, as considerably greater, and so they are able to work out the intricate characteristics of languge and its uses.

We shall not discuss these hypotheses and the evidence for and against each of them, but go on to describe what children's language is like at different stages in its development, by examining the spoken language of children under the age of four. We shall look at authentic samples of the language of children talking to their parents in the home, and for each example we shall ask the general question: What language skills enabled the child to say what he or she said, in the way he or she said it?

6.2 **Pronunciation skills** (Cassette tape, Section 16)

Firstly, some examples of a child's **pronunciation** in brief extracts from conversations between a mother and her young son, Danny. The conversations were video-recorded over a period of six months from the age of two to two and a half.

The extracts have been selected to illustrate three distinct stages of development in the six-month period.

Stage A
(1)
M. don't want the egg shell do you?
D. /ʃaɪ ʃu/ ugh.

(2)

M.   what is it? cold?

D.   /kaʊʃ/

(3)

D.   /sɪg/

M.   mm

D.   /ʃɪg/

M.   cheese?

(4)

M.   what is it Dan?

D.   /kɑk/

M.   cart (.) yes the dustcart.

Stage B

(1)

M.   mm yeah. it's a dustcart.

D.   /ə dʊskɑt/

(2)

M.   what's that?

       (2.0)

D.   /wil/

M.   yes it's a wheel (.) they've all got wheels haven't they?

(3)

D.   /lɪki kɑ lɪki kɑ/lɪki kɑ lɪki kɑ/

M.   yes that's a little car and that's a little car (.)
       so that's one little car (.) two little cars

(4)

M.   alligator

D.   /æli æligeɪti gɒt æləgeɪti/æləgeɪti ə ka /

M.   yes (.) alligator

(5)

D.   / ðaets **mok** væn/

M.   a milk van yes

Stage C

(1)

D.   /aɪ gɒt kot **bred** naʊ /

M.   cold bread

D.   mm

(2)
D. /aɪ don wɒn ə go ə wɒtʃət/
M. no (.) cos he's not there any more (.) they've moved

Naturally, we cannot, on the basis of the few examples given, give anything like a complete description of the skills relevant to pronunciation which Danny has learned or developed. But we can begin to appreciate what is involved in pronouncing even these few utterances.

(i) Sound segments

In studying pronunciation, we try to identify the **segments** of sound the child makes. Different segments have different characteristics – they are particular kinds of **vowel** or **consonant**. They are organised in certain **sequences**, together with **stress** on some syllables and movements of **pitch**.

Exercise

(a)   List the different sound segments that the child produces.
(b)   Using the symbol C for a consonant, and V for a vowel, list the kinds of consonant-vowel sequences that make up the child's words.
(c)   List the words of more than one syllable, and underline the syllables that are stressed.
(d)   Comment on the child's and the mother's different uses of intonation. Are there any patterns of pitch movement?

Commentary

In answering these questions, it is helpful to consider what the answers would be if we were studying the mother's pronunciation. For example, in the first extract illustrating Stage A in Danny's language development, the mother uses five distinct vowel sounds: /o/, /ɒ/, /ə/, /e/, /u/, whereas Danny uses only five vowels in all four Stage A extracts: /aɪ/, /u /, /aʊ/, /ɪ/, /ɑ/.
  Furthermore, Danny's vowels can be unstable. In trying to pronounce *shell* he says /ʃˈaɪ / and /ʃ u/, and in only one case does his pronunciation of a vowel match his mother's, as you can see from the following list:

word	Mother vowel	Child vowel
shell	/e/	/aɪ/ and /u /
cold	/o /	/aʊ/
cheese	/i /	/ɪ/
(dust)cart	/ɑ/	/ɑ/

So at this stage, the child can produce certain recognisable vowels, but they may vary when the child is repeating the same word, and they do not necessarily match the vowels of adult speakers.

If we then compare the **consonants** produced by Danny at Stage A and compare them with his mother's, we again find obvious differences. The following consonants occur in Danny's speech: /ʃ/, /k/, /s/, /g/. His use of them is unstable too. In pronouncing the first sound of the word *cheese* he uses both /ʃ/ and /s/, and neither of these is the same as the adult pronunciation /tʃ/. Here is a summary of the use of consonants in the Stage A extracts:

word	Mother consonant	Child consonant
shell	/ʃ – 1/	/ʃ – –/
cold	/k – ld/	/k – –/
cheese	/tʃ – z/	/s – g/ and /ʃ – g/
(dust)cart	/k – t/	/k – k/

If you examine stages B and C, you will find that Danny has learned to produce other vowels and consonants, sounds that are stable in their characteristics and also more like the corresponding adult sounds in the same words. For example, at Stage A he pronounces *shell*, which has the sound /l/ at the end, without a consonant in that position. This is perhaps because he cannot or will not pronounce the sound in **word-final** position, whereas at Stage B he is pronouncing *wheel* as /wi:l/, that is, he is now using /1/ in word-final position. You will also notice that *wheel* has the vowel /i/ in his pronunciation, although at Stage A Danny pronounced the vowel of *cheese* as /ɪ/, /ʃɪg/.

Similarly, notice that at Stage A he pronounced *dustcart* as /kɑk/, and by Stage B this has become /dʊskɑt/.

(ii) Sound sequences

Sound segments combine in various ways to form words, and we describe the sequences as combinations of consonants and vowels. If we look again at the mother's utterances in the Stage A extracts, we can represent the individual words according to their sequences of consonants (C) and vowels (V) like this:

(1)

don't	/dont/	CVCC
want	/wɒnt/	CVCC
the	/ðə/	CV
egg	/eg/	VC
do	/du/	CV
you	/ju/	CV

(2)

what	/wɒt/	CVC
is	/ɪz/	VC
it	/ɪt/	VC
cold	/kold/	CVCC

(3)

cheese	/tʃiz/	CVC

(4)

what	/wɒt/	CVC
is	/ɪz/	VC
it	/ɪt/	VC
Dan	/dæn/	CVC
cart	/kɑt/	CVC
yes	/jes/	CVC
the	/ðə/	CV
dustcart	/dʊskɑt/	CVCCVC

So the mother can produce at least the following sequences: CV, VC, CVC, CVCC, CVCCVC. And if we analysed more of her speech, it would show her capable, as we would expect, of other types of sequence – all those in fact that belong to English pronunciation. Now examine Danny's sequences of vowel and consonant at Stage A:

(1)

shell	/ʃaɪ/ and /ʃu/	CV

(2)
cold   /kaʊ/   CV
(3)
cheese   /sɪg/ and / ʃɪg/   CVC
(4)
dustcart   /kɑk/   CVC

On this evidence, Danny can only produce a limited range of sequences of sound segments at Stage A. However, the rapid progress he
makes in this aspect of language skill becomes immediately clear if you
examine the sequences in the words he produces at Stage B. Look in
particular at his pronunciation of the word *alligator* in extract (4).

(iii) Patterns of stress and pitch
Little can be said about patterns of stress placement (which syllables
carry more stress than others) at Stage A, because at this stage Danny
only produces utterances of one word, and each word is a **monosyllable**.
So neither a syllable within a word, nor any particular word in a sequence of words, can receive more or less stress than any other. However,
at Stage C, the child's use of stress is clear as we see him using stress to
foreground or emphasise particular words:

D. I got cold **bread** now

and applying stress to particular syllables in **polysyllabic** words:

D. I don't want to go to **Watch**ett

But Danny's use of **pitch** to signal differences in meaning is quite
clear from the start. Consider first how pitch is used by adult speakers.
Say the sentence 'You're coming' first as if you were asking a question,
and then as if you were answering a question. Most speakers will find
that when asking the question, the pitch level at which they are speaking begins to rise on the first syllable of *coming*; when answering a
question, the pitch level begins to fall on that syllable.
Now look at extract (4) from Stage A:

M. what is it Dan?
D. /kȃk/
M. cart (.) yes (.) the dustcart

Here what the child says is marked as having a downward pitch movement, but what he is saying is, of course, an answer to a question from his mother. Danny is thus, even at this early stage of one-word utterances, using a pitch movement to mark his utterance as having the function of an answer, in much the same way as adults do.

Now extract (3) from Stage A:

D. /sɪg/
M. mm
D. /ʃɪg/
M. cheese

In this extract the child is the first to speak. In fact he is asking for cheese, or in other words making a **request**. This time his utterance is marked as having an **upward** movement in pitch. So an upward pitch movement is associated for him with a request function. The mother, however, does not respond directly to the child's request, but queries what he has said, using what is in effect a question. Her utterance has upward pitch movement. Danny's response this time is an attempt to provide his mother with the information her question was intended to elicit, and so it is an **answer**. The same word is repeated, but with **downward** pitch movement. Thus Danny is using pitch movement in a systematic and meaningful way.

This description of Danny's skills in producing and sequencing segments of sound, and using stress and pitch, will give you some idea of the complexity of a child's task in learning how to pronounce the language. It is not complete, and you should try to apply the same systematic process of analysis to discover more for yourself.

6.3 Grammatical skills (Cassette tape, Section 17)

Children develop skills in pronunciation, of course, at the same time as they are developing knowledge of the use of words in different combinations to express meanings. This is what we refer to as a child's knowledge of the **grammar** of the language.

We shall look firstly at some examples of the speech of a linguistically advanced two-and-a-half-year-old girl, Kirsty, and then at how Danny gradually developed the knowledge of the grammar that this girl had.

6.3.1   Kirsty

(i) Sentence-types

Children learn that when words are combined with others to form *sequences*, then these sequences must conform to particular *patterns* – that is, they develop an awareness of **sentence structure types** such as **declarative**, **interrogative**, **imperative**.
Examples:

I drop Katie's skirt in Tom's playpen	= declarative mood
did you find the card for Tom?	= interrogative mood
you speak in it (i.e. the tape-recorder)	= imperative mood

(ii)   Word-classes

Children learn that words with quite different meanings can be used in similar ways. You can change the form of some words in the same way, or combine them with other words in the same way – that is, children develop an awareness of **word-classes** (or **parts of speech**) such as noun, verb, adjective.

(iii)   Grammatical roles

Children learn that, independent of their meanings, words or groups of words have certain jobs to do in a sentence – that is, they become aware of **grammatical roles** such as **subject** and **predicate**, and within the predicate, the **predicator** (or **verb**), **object** or **complement**, and **adverbial**.
Example:

S	P		O	
	(aux)	(verb)	(modifier)	(noun/pronoun)
I	going to	iron	Katie's	coat
I	going to	do	Jane's	pants
I	going to	draw	my two little	girls
I	going to	have		'tatoes
Betty	going to	have		orange
She	going to	have		juice
She	must	sit		(A) between my knees
You	must	wash		it
I	must	have		it

(iv)   Word-forms
Children learn that they can alter meaning by using a variety of processes to change the form of words – for example, they become aware of
the ways we use to show **tense** and **aspect** in the verb phrase of the
predicator, and **number** in the noun phrase of the subject, object or
complement, by adding inflections like *-ed*, *-ing*, and *-s*.
Examples:

tense	Subject	Predicator	Object or Complement	Adverbial
present (+ negative)	I	*don't* know		
past (+ negative)	I	*didn't* iron	it	
past	I	*did* hang	them	over
aspect				
perfective (+ negative)	I	*haven't* iron*ed*	that	
progressive	Tom	's play*ing*		
	I	's talk*ing*		to Tom
	they	're sitt*ing*		together
number				
singular	Tom	would like	a *straw*	
plural	I	want	some *straws*	
singular	*he*	's got	a clean jumper	
plural	*they*	're falling down		a bit
singular	*this*	is	my *crayon*	
plural	*these*	are	my *crayons*	

These short extracts from Kirsty's speech at two and a half show
you how she is already competent in some of the basic features of
English grammar.

6.3.2 Danny
We shall now look at the development of this grammatical knowledge
in Danny's speech at the three stages we have already considered when
examining his pronunciation.

Exercise

For each stage,

(a)   List the words which the child has inflected.

(b)   Indicate whether the inflected word is a noun, adjective, or verb, and give the reasons for your classifications.

(c)   List the noun phrases (NPs) used by the child which involve the use of determiners, adjectives, and other modifiers, in combination.

(d)   List examples of the child's use of simple past tense and progressive aspect in the verb phrase (VP).

(e)   List examples of his use of the negative and of interrogative mood.

(f)   List examples of his use of coordinated and subordinated clauses.

(Do not expect to find examples of all these features at every stage of the child's language development.)

Stage A

(1)

M.   do you want to open your egg?
      (3.0)
      the shell off
      don't want the egg shell do you?

D.   /ʃaɪ ʃu/ ugh

M.   the shell's not nice
      only Mr Silly in your Silly book eats the shell
      doesn't he?

D.   ugh [*laughs*]

(2)

M.   what is it? cold?

D.   /kaʊ/

M.   is it?
      put too much in // the

D.   /sɪg/

M.   mm

D.   /ʃɪg/

M.   cheese?

D.   cheese

M.   well you eat your egg first and then you can have
      some cheese

(3)
M.   who's looking // who's looking through the camera?
D.   mum
     man
M.   it's a man isn't it?
D.   /gɔ wən/
M.   Gordon (.) that's right

Stage B
(1)
M.   that isn't a number // it's a
D.   traffics
M.   traffic
D.   go
M.   traffic lights (.) yes and it means go because it's on (.) what
     colour is it? when it says? when it means go?
D.   green
M.   green
(2)
M.   what else can you see in there?
D.   more statue
M.   more statue
(3)
D.   the big long lo long long train
M.   long crane
(4)
D.   look (.) he went (winter) (.) (winterz)
M.   vintage yes (.) one two three vintage cars
D.   fast car vintage (.) fast car vintage
M.   fast car vintage
D.   fast car vintage
(5)
M.   yeah well isn't (.) what's fallen out?
D.   fall out that *man* the man // down
M.   mm down
D.   down
(6)
M.   what's he lifting? what's the crane lifting up?
D.   tractor
M.   oh it's another tractor is'nt it?

(7)

M.   what do you think it's doing if it's got brushes on the car? (0.5) what do you do with brushes?

D.   sweep (.) up

M.   sweep up

(8)

M.   what do you think he's (.) putting water on the road for?

D.   piggy
      (0.5)

M.   splashing the piggy (.) what's the water doing?

D.   splash piggy

(9)

M.   oh who's drawn on there then?

D.   Becca draw on there

M.   oh was it Rebecca?

D.   yes

(10)

M.   who's that (.) is that the daddy?

D.   no (.) Daddy sit (.) Daddy sit er er Danny sit (.) Daddy sit there

M.   he's sitting there is he? where's where where's the other family?

D.   look there's one

M.   there's some more family Danny (.) come on (.) there's the baby and a little girl (.) they're all going out to the seaside for the day (2.0)
    oh mustn't forget the Mummy (.) now who else is missing?

D.   (*) Mummy sit there

M.   Mummy sit there

D.   no not sitting (*) that's Mummy's

M.   oh yes (.) Mummy's done it wrong (.) that's the little child (.) yes that's the Mummy (.) oh I'm silly (.) oh and there's the other one

Stage C

(1)

D.   I doing like this all day

M.   come on (.) hurry up (.) I've eaten mine

D.   I do (.) I doing this all day look (.) I got a library book

M.   wha. which lib. what's your library book called?

D.   mister (*) and (*) that person er that dog

M.   that dog (.) do you know (.) can you remember what
the dog's name is?
(2.0)
called Harry isn't he?

D.   Harry

M.   mm

(2)

D.   I don't want to go to Watchett

M.   no (.) cos he's not there any more (.) they've moved

D.   I (.) we don't want go and see them

M.   M. don't you? but you'd like to go and see them in Liverpool
wouldn't you?

D.   no I don't want (.) I want to go (.) when get bigger want to go
on my own a a Watchett

M.   do you? you want to go on your own?

D.   not a bi. not a (.) when get bigger

M.   when you get bigger yes (.) you'll be able to do lots of things
when you get bigger (.) you'll perhaps be able to ride on an
aeroplane

D.   it's on (1.0) like on television

M.   mm (1.0) it showed you some children in the aeroplane on the
television didn't it?

Commentary

Stage A

The most obvious feature of the child's talk here is that he speaks in
single word utterances. The single words are, however, used to convey
a variety of messages. In A(2), /kaʊs/ = *cold* is used to label a quality.
In A(3), *man* is used to label a sort of being to be found in the world,
and /gɔwən/ = *Gordon* is used to label a specific being in the child's
world.

    Can we then say that the child has sets of words for doing one sort
of thing, like labelling persons? If we did, then we could use the terms
from the description of English grammar, like adjective, noun, proper
noun etc. But there are two problems if we do this:

(i)   The child's 'single words' are not simply used as labels for things,
qualities, people, and actions. As well as this use, in A(1) /ʃaɪ ʃu/
= *shell* is used as part of an expression of disgust. In A2 /sɪg/ *and*
/ʃɪg/ = *cheese* is used to express a request.

    Any one 'word' can be used for a variety of purposes by the child. On one occasion he may say / ʃɪg/ to ask for some cheese, but on another simply to label it.

(ii) There is no way of distinguishing sets of words other than by the purpose for which they are used, and this, as we have seen, can vary with particular occasions of use. Adults and children know that *Gordon* belongs to a different set from *man*, because we can say *the man*, but can't say *the Gordon*. Similarly, we know that *cold* belongs to a different set from *cheese*, because we can say, for example, *colder*, but not *cheeser*. But Danny, at this stage, only uses words in isolation, and never alters their form.

  At Stage A, therefore, the child's language does not seem to involve any **structural** organisation.

Stage B

Stage B shows considerable development in the child's language. He is now combining words into sequences. Extracts (1) to (4) show that it now makes sense to talk of the child's awareness of different sets of words, even though he makes mistakes in classifying them.

  In B(1) Danny applies a **plural marker** to the word *traffic*, which suggests that he knows something about the category **noun**.

  In B(2) he does not apply the plural marker to the word *statue*, where the context would require it. This suggests that although he has begun to learn the difference between **count** and **non-count** nouns (e.g. *statues* and *traffic*), he has not yet mastered it.

  In B(3), *long* is correctly placed in front of *train*; in B(4), *vintage* is wrongly placed after the noun *car*. This suggests that he has an emerging but not yet complete awareness of the category **adjective** and its place in the structure of the noun phrase.

  B(5) shows an awareness of the **grammatical role** or function of the **subject** of a clause. In the question asked by Danny's mother, the word *what* is the subject of the clause.

  In B(6), the word *what* in the question is the grammatical **object** in the clause. In B(7) and (8), the question is asking for an answer which supplies the **predicate** of the clause:

brushes	sweep up	the water	splashes Piggy
Subject	*Predicate*	*Subject*	*Predicate*

B(9) and (10) show Danny using well-formed sentences, where everything that should be there is in place. In B(9), he is showing his understanding of **location** and uses a **prepositional phrase**, *on there* to show it. B(10) shows that he can distinguish different **mood** structures and uses them:

declarative mood:	Daddy sit there	that's Mummy's
imperative mood:	look	

He can obviously understand **interrogative** structures as questions and answer them. He is beginning to use **progressive aspect** in the predicator:

no not sit*ting*

although he does not yet use the verb *be* as part of it, as in:

no Mummy *is*n't sit*ting* there

This clause also shows his understanding of the **negative** particle *not*.

Stage C
You can see clearly that Stage C is the most adult-like of Danny's language, even though things that you would expect in adult speech are still missing.

C(1) and (2) show Danny using **determiners** – words that come first in a noun phrase and refer to definiteness and indefiniteness (like *a*, *the*, *this*, *some*, *each*, *much*, etc.):

all day   *a* library book   *that* dog   on *my* own

This allows Danny to be more specific in the references he makes.

He is again using progressive aspect in the verb phrase, and still hasn't learned to use the auxiliary verb *be*:

I do*ing* this

He can use the negative, as before, and is now also using the auxiliary verb *do* with it:

I *don't* want

Before this stage, he would have said 'I *no* want' or 'I *not* want'.

He is using more complex verb phrases, with **finite** and **non-finite** forms of the verb:

I don't *want to go*

He can **inflect** an adjective to make the **comparative** form:

when get *bigger*

He constructs prepositional phrases which are not to do with place or location:

on my own

Perhaps the most significant development at Stage C is Danny's use of **subordination**, when one clause is dependent on, or embedded in another clause. This modifies the meaning of whole sentence structures:

[when get bigger]   want to go on my own a Watchett
subordinate adverbial   *main clause*
clause

This rather detailed description of what Danny 'knows' about the grammar of English helps to explain what was meant in the third paragraph of this chapter: 'If we consider just what goes on when children learn their first language, we can begin to appreciate the true nature and complexity of the skills which they have.'

We all know the grammar of English in the sense of *implicit knowledge* because we are all fluent speakers of the language. This little study of Danny's speech may help you to know the grammar in a more explicit way also.

6.4 Discourse and conversation skills (Cassette tape, Section 18)

Children learn and use their knowledge of the pronunciation and grammar of the language in the course of conversation. But to participate in conversation in a way that appears to be competent and natural requires skills that go beyond the ability to produce well-articulated grammatical sequences of words. These skills are referred to as **conversation** or **discourse** skills. They underly a child's ability to engage and then hold the attention of those she is speaking to by:

1. taking turns at speaking in ways which produce smoothly flowing conversations;
2. saying things which follow on from, or fit in with what others in the conversation are saying; and
3. constructing utterances in ways which successfully achieve what the child intends, in relation to the other speakers in the conversation.

We can again examine Danny's language at different stages of his development to find out the extent to which he has learned these skills.

6.4.1   Turn-taking

Look again at Stage **A**, extract (2). There is a clear pattern here of alternating speakers, and so there is some form of **turn-taking**. However, if we look more closely we can see that the taking of turns differs from that in conversations of speakers who are more linguistically mature.

The sequence starts with a question directed to Danny. Before Danny's response the mother provides what is in effect the appropriate content for Danny's turn. Danny then takes the turn, using the material his mother has already provided for him, that is, the word *cold*. It is quite common in conversations between children and adults at this stage to find the mother consciously avoiding gaps in the conversation. She will deal with likely 'non-responses' by incorporating into her own turn material that would be an appropriate response for the child.

The mother's next speaking turn is not completed before the child begins to speak:

M.   put too much in // the
D.   / s ɪg/

The child here starts to speak at a point when the mother's utterance is grammatically incomplete. She has produced only the preposition *in* of what is to be a prepositional phrase. One of the ways of timing the beginning of a speaking turn is to listen for points of grammatical completeness in the other speaker's turn. This is what Danny seems to fail to do.

The following illustration from Kirsty's speech at two and a half illustrates well that children can quite quickly come to monitor for grammatical completeness:

M. no he doesn't have that milk in the packets any more he drinks
   the same milk as you doesn't he?
K. mm
M. out of a
K. cup
M. and the milkman brings it in a
K. house
M. yes he brings it to the house

Notice here that the child is monitoring the mother's speech sufficiently closely to be able to provide a word of just the right grammatical class to make the mother's utterance complete.

Children also become aware that gaps between turns are to be avoided, and that if they do occur, then something might be wrong – that is, the gap takes on some sort of meaning. Consider the following exchange between a mother and three-year-old:

C. I'm gonna buy eight yoghurt
M. eight?
C. yeah
   (1.0)
   is that a lot?

Here the mother queries the child's first utterance by repeating part of what he said, and he confirms the mother's repetition. Normally at this point you would expect the mother to continue the topic in some way, or at the very least to say something. But for a full second, which is a long time in conversation, she says nothing. The child then continues with a question, 'is that a lot?' which implies that he interprets the mother's silence as suggesting that something was wrong with his original assertion.

We can see from these examples that as they learn to organise their turn-taking in conversation, children are able to avoid gaps between turns and overlapping of turns.

6.4.2 Coherence, or fitting-in

Conversation, of course, involves more than just taking turns at speaking. What is said must fit in with what has gone before, and its relevance must be apparent to each speaker. In the very early stages of language development it is rare for talk to be focused on a topic for more than three or four speaking turns. The child simply doesn't have the linguistic resources to do this. We can see something of the resources involved in maintaining talk over several turns by considering the following extract:

Mother and Stephanie

M.	do you know how old you'll be?
S.	well (.) how old
M.	well how old are you now?
S.	/fri/
M.	so next birthday you'll be? 5
	(2.0)
S.	four
M.	four
S.	yes (.) I like being four don't we?
M.	do you like being four? 10
S.	yes (.) bu.(.h) but w. after when Geoffrey's /bin/
	four how old will he be?
M.	what do you think?
S.	five
M.	yes 15
S.	and then how old?
M.	and then he'll be six
S.	and then how old will me?
M.	and then you'll be five won't you?
S.	and then it won't be our birthday(s) will it? 20
	(1.0)
	and it will be /stev/ won't it?
M.	mm
S.	we we're have plenty of birthdays aren't we?
M.	I hope so 25
S.	but Father Christmas brung bringded our toys didn't he?
M.	mm
	(1.0)

	he doesn't bring you toys on your birthday does he?	30
S.	but after our birthday(s) (.) gonna (.) Christmas	
	going to come but he but he won't eat a (.h) he (.)	
	tart (.) he'll just leave one	
M.	one tart	
S.	yes (.) you've made one	35
M.	did we leave him a tart last Christmas?	
S.	yes	
	(2.0)	
M.	do you like tarts?	
S.	mm	40
	(1.0)	
	but (.) but once (.) we couldn't eat some could we?	
M.	why not?	
S.	that's why they were (.) a bit stiff couldn't we?	
M.	a bit stiff!	45
S.	yes	
M.	oh	
S.	yes but you said they were didn't you?	
M.	oh I see	

Here both mother and child contribute to the creation of coherent
discourse through the use of question-answer routines, continuers,
lexical repetition, **deixis**, and question tags.

(i)   Question-answer routines

These ensure topic responses and can be maintained over as many turns
as you like, since any question can have another question as an answer.
On this basis the first six turns can be analysed as:

M.	Q. do you know how old you'll be?
S.	Q. well (.) how old?
M.	Q. well how old are you now?
S.	A. /fri/
M.	Q. so next birthday you'll be?
	(2.0)
S.	A. four

(ii)   Continuers

These serve to treat what is to be said in some current speaking turn as following on in some logical way from what has been said in a previous turn. Often the logical link is signalled by some grammatical device:

S.   **and then** how old?
M.   **and then** he'll be six
S.   **and then** how old will me?
M.   **and then** you'll be five won't you?
S.   **and then** it won't be our birthday(s) will it?   5
     (1.0)
     and it will be /stev/ won't it?
M.   mm
S.   we we're have plenty of birthday's aren't we?
M.   I hope so   10
S.   **but** Father Christmas brung bringded our toys didn't
     he?
M.   mm
     (1.0)
     he doesn't bring toys on your birthday does he?   15
S.   **but after** our birthday(s) (.) gonna (.) Christmas
     going to come

The items in bold type are clear indications that the turns they preface are 'on-topic' continuations.

(iii)   Lexical repetition

This is a most basic method of linking turns and there are many examples in the extract:

M.   so next birthday you'll be?
     (2.0)
S.   **four**
M.   **four**
S.   yes (.) I like being **four** don't we?   5
M.   do you like being **four**?

(iii)   Deixis

Deixis literally means *pointing*, and refers to the way in which speakers can use certain words to point to, rather than name, things already mentioned in a conversation. We use pronouns in this way. For example:

S.   but **Father Christmas** brung bringded our toys didn't
     he?
M.   mm
     (1.0)
     he doesn't bring you toys on your birthday does **he**?   5
S.   but after our birthday(s) (.) gonna (.) **Christmas**
     going to come but **he** but **he** won't eat a (.h) **he** (.)
     tart **he**'ll just leave one

The relevance of the mother's turn and the child's second turn to
her own first turn is maintained by the **deictic** use of pronouns to refer
to Father Christmas.

(iv)   Question tags

Question tags do not necessarily function as requests for information,
but have as a primary role the establishment of an obligation to respond.
This can be done in other ways, for example, the use of terms of address
as in, 'I like being four **mum**'. It would be odd not to respond to this.

However, both speakers here use question tags as a way of ensuring
'listener response':

S.   we we're have plenty of birthdays **aren't we**?
M.   I hope so

6.4.3   Response to other speakers' needs

(i)   What they want to know

Children become increasingly sensitive to the different ways in which
messages need to be constructed. In the early stages children don't have
the resources to adjust their messages to take account of their listener's
needs and expectations. But look at the following extract from Danny's
speech at his Stage 3. He is responding to a question, and we can see
him adjusting the way he refers to something in order to make his
answer more specific, and so provide a better chance of satisfying the
presumed 'informational needs' of his mother, that is, what she wants
to know:

M.   wha. which lib. what's your library book called?
D.   Mister (*) and (*)
     that person er that the dog

(ii)   Politeness
Children also learn to take account of such things as the need for
politeness in constructing their requests:

C.   want a bic bic
M.   pa:rdon?
       (1.5)
C.   I would *like* a bic bic
M   *that's* better
C.   please

The ways of showing politeness in requests are of course many, and
range from the use of lexical items like *please* to complex syntactic
constructions like *I was wondering if you would mind awfully* . . .

Whilst all children have much in common, there will always be
interesting differences between them in the way that they speak at any
stage of development. Their pronunciation, grammar, and ability to use
language in conversation will be the special product of each child's
experience of language. Any investigation you do of any child's language
will be your own original research.

7

Variety and style in spoken English

If we consider the range of situations in which language is used, the many kinds of people with whom we communicate, and the different purposes for which we talk or write, the task of describing all the varieties of English usage proves very daunting. To create some kind of order in studying variety in language use, a framework of concepts is taken from **linguistics** (the systematic study of language).

Think of the English language as a **system** that we have all learned and carry around in our minds. Whenever we talk or write, we have to make choices from this system, which gives us a number of alternatives at each linguistic level, including choices of words from our **vocabulary**, and different ways of putting these words together in 'strings' called **sentences**.

Our sentences must obey the rules which everyone who speaks English follows. Dialects of a language share the same rules except for a small number which differ slightly. The words must be in the right order to be **grammatical**, but again there is enough flexibility to allow a lot of choice.

Our vocabulary and grammar must be in the right **style**, or **appropriate** to the context, as well as grammatically correct. Usually we fall into the right style without really knowing what makes it right, but we do make mistakes. We can also use the wrong style deliberately if we want to.

What follows, in the next three chapters on variety and style, is a selected series of texts, spoken and written, which are clearly distinctive varieties of English. They are chosen partly because they are familiar and important varieties, and partly because they contrast with each other. The commentaries try to show, as explicitly as possible, how to make a descriptive analysis of a text.

The terminology from linguistics is used, as in the preceding chapters, to identify those features of the texts which distinguish them from other varieties. You cannot easily describe a flower garden without naming the flowers.

Sometimes the most prominent features of style are those which are the most frequent - there seem to be a lot of them. The problem is, how to judge at what point the number of features is 'more frequent' than usual. Nevertheless, we do recognise stylistic features as being typical or unusual, from our everyday experience as speakers of English.

7.1   Bedtime stories (Cassette tape, Section 19)

7.1.1   Susan's narrative

Here are a few minutes taken from a narrative spoken by a five-year-old girl, and shared with another girl of the same age. They were both in the reception class of a York infants' school, and were talking to an adult for about an hour altogether, on all kinds of topics that came into their minds. The subject of 'bedtime' occupied them for a long time.

The transcription is into ordinary spelling, and does not attempt to show intonation, stress, or regional accent.

```
my Mummy's got (.) two pillows (.) one on top and one
underneath (.) and then she's got em (.) my Dad's got two
(.) one (.) and er he puts his head under the pillow
because there's a em (.) a sla. a slat (.) and he puts his
head under the pillow and then he goes to sleep (.) he          5
covers hisself up and my Mummy chucks the em (.) covers
down the side here (.) and em sometimes I don't have my
bed chucked in but I like (.) and then er (.) sometimes
Alan won't go to bed because (.) sometimes when we put him
to bed and I go to bed he cries (.) and he thought ooh         10
this is a good idea he gets out of bed and walks (.)
walks back into the room (.) [giggles] cos he's in a bed
like me now he used to go in his carry-cot (.) but when we
was going to get another one I slept in the carry-cot (.)
[giggles] and then (.) we've got another we've got a bed        15
now (.) and then every night when we put him to bed (.) he gets
up and goes into the room somet. (.) sometimes he walks if you put
him to bed (.) and then he walks (.) and I thought ooh
I'll go back (.) daren't go in the room (.) then he tries
```

again (.) so (.) I'll go back (.) he'll never go in the   20
room (.) so (.) my Mum's heard him going trip trap in his
bare feet because he can't put his (.) blue slippers on
yet they're like mine (.) em and then (.) and then (.) she
said 'come on in' and then when he gets into the room my
Mum says he's a naughty boy because he (.) I go to bed   25
before him you see because er (.) I want to go to bed and
sometimes when I'm tired I go (.) I don't go to bed (.)
one time I went when it was (.) half past nine (.) and it
was nearly half past ten when I went to bed (.)

Exercise 1

List and describe some of the normal non-fluency features of the girl's
speech (see chapter 5).

(These features do not identify the special characteristics of Susan's
language use. But it is useful to examine them and to consider their
function.)

Exercise 2

Examine the transcript for non-standard vocabulary and grammar (see
chapter 3).

If you do this systematically, some distinguishing features will
become evident, which will help you to confirm Susan's language as
(i) dialectal, and (ii) a child's.

Exercise 3

Edit the text by leaving out the non-fluency features. Then write it out
clause by clause, and group the clauses into clause-complexes (spoken
sentences).

The criteria for grouping the clauses are:

(i)   **prosodic** – the meaning conveyed by intonation, stress and pauses,
(ii)   **grammatical** – the meaning conveyed by the relationship between
       clauses, phrases and words, and
(iii) **semantic** – the meaning of words and the topics she chooses to
       talk about.

To show how this can be done, here is the beginning of the clause /
clause-complex analysis.

Column (a)   = coordinating conjunctions
Column (b)   = subordinating conjunctions
Column (c)   = initial adverbials (adverbials which precede the subject,
and so are thematic in the clause)

1. (a)   (b)   (c)
                                my Mummy's got two pillows, one on top
                                and one underneath

2. and   then   she's got [*unfinished*]

3.   my Dad's got one

4. and   he puts his head under the pillow
5.   because   there's a slat
6. and   he puts his head under the pillow
7. and   then   he goes to sleep

8.   he covers hisself up
9. and   my Mummy chucks the covers down the
                                side here

10. and   sometimes I don't have my bed chucked in
11. but   I like   [*unfinished*]

12. and   then   Alan won't go to bed
                        sometimes
13.   because   [*unfinished*]

14.   sometimes he cries
15.   when   we put him to bed
16. and ∅   I go to bed
17. and   he thought
18.   ooh this is a good idea

19.		he gets out of bed
20.	and	Ø walks back into the room
21.	cos	he's in a bed like me now
22.		he used to go in his carry-cot
23.	but	I slept in the carry-cot
24.	when	we was going to get another one

Commentary

(i)   Non-standard forms

What is of most interest in Susan's talk is the frequency of non-standard English forms, and aspects of her language use which appear typical of a child. We shall identify and discuss these in some detail. (The figures refer to the lines of the transcription.)

(4)   *because there's a slat* – she uses *because* or *cos* several times, some of them without any real casual relation being implied. Here she does not convey her full meaning, but assumes that her listener can infer the connection between the slat and Dad putting his head under the pillow.

(6)   *hisself* – dialectal (cf. chapter 3)

(6)   *chucks* – dialectal, or family usage?

(7)   *down the side here* – by using *here*, she is not yet distancing what she describes from the immediate context. She is not talking beside Dad's bed. Our vocabulary and grammar provide the means of 'pointing' to time, place and people (**deixis** and **deictic** features, see chapter 6). But deictic features can only be understood if the listener knows the context.

(10)   *and he thought* – notice her tendency to use both present and past tenses in her narrative, not always consistently related.

(12)   *the room* – means specifically what elsewhere would be called *the living-room*.

(14)   *we was going to get* – dialectal past tense of *be*.

(21–3)   this sequence is typical of much of her narrative in its apparent lack of relevance. She links ideas connected in her mind by experience, but she has yet to learn to explain the connection to a listener. The reference to the colour of Alan's slippers, and the fact that they are like hers, shows the importance to her of facts which older children and adults would either explain in more detail, or omit.

(ii)   Clauses and clause-complexes

The criteria (prosodic, grammatical, and semantic) for dividing the transcript into clause-complexes are sometimes contradictory. For example, if *and* often occurs at the beginning of a spoken sentence but after a pause, then the rule for written English that two clauses joined by *and* belong inside the same sentence may not apply.

Pauses are not always reliable in marking the division between sentences, and occur for a number of different reasons within the clauses and phrases.

So to try to identify a spoken sentence we have to rely on a combination of clues from meaning (for example, we expect a sentence to express one topic), grammar, and prosodic features. Even then, a decision will sometimes have to be an arbitrary choice, and we will not agree with each other's analysis. The idea of *sentence* in spoken English, as we have seen in chapter 5, is 'fuzzy'.

(iii)   The structure of a five-year-old child's language

The structure of Susan's language and the relationship between the clauses, which are the successive **propositions** or statements she is making, show some interesting features.

(a)   Linkage: Notice the expected frequency of *and* as a **continuer**, often followed by the adverb *then* to show sequencing.

(b)   Subordination: **Subordinate clauses** make **complex sentences**, and Susan uses *when* to indicate time, *because* to indicate a reason, and *if* to express a condition. These are **subordinating conjunctions**. She uses *so*, a **conjunct**, to show a result.

These all represent her developing understanding of how things happen, even though it is still limited in expression. In the talk not transcribed here she also uses *till*, but only once in an hour's conversation. Some common conjunctions which she did not use are: *while, after, before, although*.

So you can see that she still has some way to go in her **productive** use of language. It is likely, however, that she would understand these conjunctions in someone else's speech, in her **receptive** use of language.

In assessing a variety or style of English we have to take into account what is not there, as much as what is.

(c)   Theme: One quite frequent feature of her talk is the placing of an

adverbial of time, usually *sometimes*, at the beginning of a clause, where it becomes prominent. This placing of an item at the front of a clause is called **theme**. The adverbial is **thematic** in the clause.

(d)   Verb phrase: The **predicator** of a clause is always a verb or verb phrase (VP). VPs can be complex in adult language (e.g. I *might have been going to try to see* . . .), but in children's use of language they are still relatively simple. Complexity of the VP is a good measure of a developed use of English. The most complex of Susan's VPs in the short extracts used in this chapter are:

used to go / used to have / used to say / was going to get

Elsewhere in the conversation she says:

I've been playing / I've been doing

in which both the **perfective** (with *have*) and the **progressive** (with *be*) are combined. We also find combinations such as:

I went out skipping	*I* try to put
I want to go	*We* went to fetch
he helps to build	*he* started to go to sleep

and other series of predicators, linked one to the other as if in a chain. This kind of structure is called **catenative**, which means 'connected like links in a chain'.

The following examples of catenatives are slightly different. The subject of the second verb is not the same as the subject of the first, and so comes between them:

We wouldn't like *it* to trot around
My Mum's heard *him* going
He had *his foot* bended
my Mummy will let *him* come

The distinctive style of Susan's language can therefore be partly identified with her use of non-standard English, both dialectal and immature, and partly described in terms of simpler forms of sentence and clause structure. The topics she chose to talk about were, naturally,

related to her immediate experiences, and so determine the vocabulary
she uses.

Exercise 4

Identify what is non-standard in the following sentences, and then group
the utterances into sets containing the same features. These sentences
are taken from the complete conversation between the two children
and the teacher.)

More examples of non-standard forms in the children's language

1. Alan was kicking me. He had his foot bended like this.
2. When we was came to a corner . . .
3. If I switch my blanket off there's got a switch and you switch
   it up.
4. When he came home from work he give me a new one.
5. My Dad went to work last morning.
6. He's drawed on thingy at window – he's drawed on it – all with
   my red pen what I got for Christmas.
7. One time I put a pillow that way and sleeped on it.
8. I always had a thingy what you had to not talk with it in your
   mouth. (in answer to a question, 'What sort of thing happens
   in hospital?')
9. My Dad said when he gets a load of money, because they
   haven't got many money you see yet and so when they've got
   a load of money they're going to get a big boiler.
10. I didn't like going in Uncle Ronnie's car because it steams up
    but it doesn't now.

Exercise 5

No reference has so far been made to Susan's regional accent. Listen
again to the tape-recording, and describe some of the marked features
of her pronunciation, using the methods described in chapter 4.

Exercise 6

(a)   Listen to section 20 of the tape-recording, which continues Susan's narrative.

(b)   Comment on and explain these items from her talk:
   (i)   the use of *my* in the phrase *my Alan*.
   (ii)   the function of *the* in *in the bed*.
   (iii)   *through the lino*.
   (iv)   *he never go*.
   (v)   *a blanket what popped in a plug* and *the thingy what makes the engine warm had broke down*.
   (vi)   the sequence from *I used to have a blanket* to *but it wasn't now*.
   (vii) *we went to fetch the round ring on the car so the policeman could see it*.
   (viii) the incident with the tractor.
   (ix)   red and blue grandma.

Continuation of Susan's narrative

my Alan sometimes sleeps in the bed if he don't want to go
is his own bed (.) [*coughs*] (.) my Mum won't (.) well we
want (.) my Mummy will let him come in his (.) my bed (.) but
(.) last last night em my Daddy tried to put him in bed
(.) oh no (.) he goes through the lino back into the room   5
(.) oh no (.) he never go in my bed (.) last time (.) my
Mummy put him in my bed and er he never (.) he never em
(.) he (.) he wanted to come out (.) cos he (.) cos he doesn't
like sleeping in my bed because (.) I've got (.) I used to
have a (.) blanket what popped in a plug and we've put it (.)   10
in Alan's now because my Mummy's sleeping in the big
bedroom now (.) and er they used to say it was going to be
mine but it wasn't now and em (.) my Dad knows this one
(.) he's called Bricky and er he goes to do bricks and er
(.) and then he (.) and then he helped to (.) build it and   15
Bricky's got another boy and er sometimes (.) but last week
when we went out (.) em we went to (.) fetch the round
ring on the car so the policeman would see it and er we
couldn't because it was open at half past one and er my
Daddy only came home nearly at tea-time and then em (.)   20
and then when we got [*coughs*] got some catkins (.) em (.)

it was nearly (.) we was there and we stopped (.) my Dad
switched (.) thingy up and then he had a look at (.) well
the thingy what makes the engine warm (.) had broke down
em my Daddy wouldn't (.) when he was came to a corner when   25
we was going to go (.) straight or not em (.) he went
straight past and my Mummy (.) she didn't like going
straight past because they didn't (.) my Daddy didn't know
there was a (.) straight field where the tractor could
come straight and then straight and go through the field   30
but em he didn't look very far and then he turned (.) it
took us to grandma's but (.) we was going to go to blue
grandma's you see and em (.) we didn't go but we went to
the shop near my red grandma's (.) and then when we came
back from the shop we went to red grandma's (.) then blue   35
grandma's
[*adult*: who's red grandma and blue grandma?]
em (.) my blue grandma didn't want a blue door but she's
got a blue door (.) she had a red one before (.) and
my red (.) and my red grandma *had* a red door (.) they both   40
had a red door (.) and now they've both *got* (.) a blue
door
[*adult*: how do you know which is which?]
because er (.) we can tell (.) we can tell because they're
(.) they don't live in the both street you see   45

7.2 Unscripted commentary

7.2.1. Goal! (Cassette tape, Section 21)

Broadcasters on television and radio sometimes use scripts – texts which
are written to be read aloud – but may also have to speak off the cuff.
One of the commonest examples of this technique is **unscripted commentary**. The commentator describes and comments upon an event as
it is taking place.

The big difference between TV and radio commentary is obvious –
the TV viewer can see what's going on, but the radio listener cannot,
and the radio commentator has to provide everything that is necessary
for our understanding and enjoyment of the event in words. Some
commentators talk continuously, even on television.

Although commentators have individual styles, they have a great deal in common in their use of English, which is why unscripted commentary can be described as a variety of spoken English.

The example which follows consists of the same short period of an international soccer match between England and Belgium, described by television and radio commentators.

Radio commentary

and again it's Wilkins high across the area looking for
Keegan Keegan gets the header in (.) not enough power (.)
Ceulemans fortunately for Belgium is there to clear (.)
not very far though (.) Sansom comes forward a yard in
from the near touchline the England left (.) long ball   5
from Sansom high across the area Pfaff is there (.)
punches the ball away (.) not very far but effectively
(1.0) and Cools the (.) Belgian captain picks it up in
space (.) far side from us the Belgian left (.) he's
tackled fiercely though (.) and he loses the ball to   10
Copple (.) to Brooking (.) tall Brooking (.) of West Ham
(.) touches the ball on (.) Wilkins (.) good ball too to
Brooking (.) Brooking got four red-shirted Belgians around
him (.) turns the ball back to Keegan (.) England's
captain (.) Keegan holds (.) still holds then starts to   15
move forward slowly (.) goes away from van Moer's tackle
(.) another tackle comes in on Keegan though (.) and in
any case it's (.) a a (.) a foul tackle this time (.) plus
a handball I think (.) so it's a free kick to England (.)
this is halfway inside the Belgian half (.) England nil   20
Belgium nil (.) the opening game (.) of this group for
both these sides (.) and again (.) cries of 'England'
ringing round the stadium Wilkins takes the free kick
short to Brooking (.) five yards outside the Belgian
penalty area (.) good running by Brooking (.) down to the   25
bye-line (.) cuts the ball back (.) Meeuws is there to
head the ball away (.) not very far Wilkins trying to get
the shot in Wilkins going forward a chance for Wilkins
here (.) and Wilkins (.) has scored for England (.) oh a
most intelligent goal (.) by Ray Wilkins   30

Television commentary

Wilkins (2.0)
Keegan up (6.0)
to Sansom (2.0)
goalkeeper's coming and Johnson's up there with him (.)
and it was a reasonably good punch by er Pfaff he found   5
one of his own players and got the danger cleared (3.0)
Copple (.) so tenacious in the tackle (.) Brooking (2.0)
Wilkins (2.0)
Brooking (2.0)
Keegan (7.0)   10
and Keegan trying to take two of them on and a handball I
suspect against van der Elst (4.0)
Phil Thompson this time has made his way forward for the
free kick on the far side (2.0)
Watson has stayed back (5.0)   15
Wilkins to Brooking (7.0)
away by Meeuws (1.0) van der Elst (.) Wilkins (.) well
done by Ray Wilkins can he finish it? (1.0) oh I say (1.0)
Ray Wilkins scores for England and a cooler goal you
couldn't wish to see look at that (.) he lobbed it over   20
the defence and then over the goal-keeper . . . .

(i)   Vocabulary

The following lists of words from the commentaries are related to
soccer football, but not all of them are exclusive to soccer. Set phrases,
or **collocations**, are included, since they often link two or more common
words together to provide a technical term. For example, the words
free and *kick* have many uses in ordinary speech and writing, but put
together as *free kick* in the context of a soccer match they form a
lexical item with a special meaning. We use the term *lexical item* to
refer to single words also.

Exercise 1

How far are the following lexical items confined to the vocabulary of
soccer, and how far do they belong to other sports or activities?
   Which of them have different meanings in other contexts of use?
Try putting them into sentences where their meaning is changed.

For example: I found a bird with a broken *left wing*.
The *offside* front *wing* of my car was dented.

You will find it very helpful to use a dictionary.

goal	the left	holds	long ball
left wing	full back	come up	robbed
possession	Belgian half	brought down	free kick
defender	referee	tackle	the area
offside	off the ball	penalty area	white line
header	to clear	touchline	punches away
in space	foul	handball	lobbed
bye-line	goalkeeper	linesman	goalkeeper

Notice how the naming of places and of people is also 'context bound'. *West Ham* and *Southampton* do not refer to places but to football clubs with managers, players, and fans. Keegan and Brooking were, at the time, national figures in the sporting pages of newspapers.

(ii)   Grammatical features
If we first discover those typical features which the two transcriptions have in common, we can then compare other examples of unscripted commentary to see whether we have identified a variety which has its own rules.

It is usual to take Standard English as the norm for comparison. Remember that it is a written standard, and that the idea of appropriateness is essential in judging a variety of language in its context of use.

The problem of identifying what a sentence is in spoken English has already been discussed (chapter 5). Unscripted commentary has its own kind of **clause** structure. The beginning of the radio commentary is set out below to show the structure of its clauses more clearly. A clause which makes a statement (a **declarative** clause) will contain a **subject** (S) (usually a noun phrase, NP), and a **predicator** (P), (always a verb phrase, VP), and, depending upon its meaning, one or more **objects** (O) or **complements** (C), and one or more **adverbials** (A).

Column (a) contains coordinators, column (b) subordinators, and column (c) linking adverbs (**adjuncts**) or thematic adverbials.

(a)	(b)	(c) S	P	O/C	A
1. and	again	it	's	Wilkins	
		(Wilkins)	∅	∅	high across the area
2.			looking for	Keegan	
3.		Keegan	gets	the header	in
4.		∅	∅ not	enough power	
5.		Ceulemans	is to clear		there fortunately for Belgium
6.		∅	∅ not		very far though

Exercise 2

(a) Complete the clause analysis of the radio commentary.
(b) Describe what is unusual about the grammatical structure.

Commentary on the clause analysis

(i) Deletion of clause elements

When you try to fit the clauses of the commentary into the SPOA pattern, you find that elements are frequently not there, yet the meaning is perfectly clear in spite of this. Are these clauses really incomplete? Should we think of commentary as having its own grammar?

We can derive the incomplete clauses of the commentary from complete ones which might be spoken in different circumstances. For example:

and again it's Wilkins high across the area looking for Keegan

could be expanded into the statement,

and again it's Wilkins *who kicks/passes the ball* high across the *penalty* area, looking for Keegan

where *looking for Keegan* means *aiming for* or something like it.
Frequently the commentator makes a statement like,

not enough power	not very far though
long ball from Sansom	good ball too to Brooking

These can all be expanded into complete sentences by adding *That was/ is. . .* or *There was/ is. . .* We can say that some clause elements have been **deleted**. The commentator presents an action, pointing to its existence as a fact. He states the fact without the preliminary **existential** *there*. It has become conventional for this style to be used in most unscripted commentary.

You can compare it with the headlines of newspapers (cf. chapter 8), or with that of telegrams, in both of which **grammatical**, or **function** words are deleted because of either restricted space (headlines) or the need to save expense (telegrams).

Exercise 3

Fill in some of the **deletions** in the two commentaries so that they make acceptable Standard English clauses. Note what you have to add or alter.

(ii) Tense in the predicator

(a) Present tense: Commentators describe what is going on as they speak. Therefore they tend to use the **simple present tense** a lot:

Keegan *gets* the header in
he *loses* the ball to Copple

Exercise 4

List some other examples of the simple present tense.

(b) Other tenses: It may seem obvious that we should use the present tense for actions that are taking place in the present time, but in fact we rarely use it in ordinary conversation. We are more likely to use the

present progressive tense, of which there are some examples in the commentaries:

Wilkins *trying* to get the shot in

When referring back to an incident which has taken place, then a commentator will use the **simple past tense**:

he *found* one of his own players

or perhaps the **present perfect tense**:

Watson *has stayed* back

Occasionally the commentator may have to refer to something about to happen, and so will use the **modal auxiliary verb** *will*, or *be going to* to express the future (example from an earlier part of the commentary):

so again England *will try*

Exercise 5

List the VPs (verb phrases) and find out which tense is the most frequently used.

(iii)   Omission of be *from the predicator*
One word is often omitted in unscripted commentary. Here are some examples:

cries of 'England' Ø ringing round the stadium
Wilkins Ø going forward

The deleted word is the verb *be*, and whether it is the **main verb** or an **auxiliary** in the verb phrase of the predicator, it is often left out.

Exercise 6

List the clauses containing the verb *be* in the predicator, and those in which *be* is deleted.

(iv)   Subject and object noun phrases
As part of the job of providing interesting comment and information, the commentator will do more than just name a player:

e.g.   *Cools* the Belgian captain
        Keegan England's captain

in which the **proper noun**, the name of the player, is followed by an identifying NP (noun phrase) in **apposition** to it, or:

   tall *Brooking* of West Ham

where the name of the player is the **head word** of an expanded NP, with **modifiers**. Most of the subject NPs in the commentaries are proper nouns, with or without modifiers.

(v)   Adverbials
The high frequency of **adverbials** is another marked feature of this style. It arises from the purpose of commentary in describing when, where, and how events are taking place, because it is one of the main functions of adverbs and adverbials to express time, place, and manner.

(vi)   Theme
This is mentioned because it was a marked feature of Susan's talk in *Bedtime Stories*. In the unscripted commentary texts, however, adverbials are rarely brought to the front of the clause. Can you suggest a reason?

(vii)   Coordination of clauses
The relative infrequency of *and* as a clause coordinator or continuer is in contrast with Susan's talk, and so with ordinary conversational usage.

(viii)   Subordination
In the two transcripts, there are no subordinate **adverbial clauses**, that is, clauses beginning with *because*, *when*, or *as*, though we have noted the frequency of adverbials within the clause. Why is this?

(c)   Fluency: Listening to broadcast commentary, you will find very few examples of the normal non-fluency which we expect to accompany conversational narrative. Hesitations, self-corrections, false starts, incomplete utterances, and fillers are rarely heard. This suggests that

unscripted commentary is an acquired skill, and that though it sounds spontaneous, it has to be learned and practised.

It would be difficult to find another variety of spoken English which resembles it in style: a series of simple declarative clauses, with few coordinators, frequent deletion, a high proportion of adverbials and an unusual degree of fluency in delivery.

It does not follow, of course, that all other radio and television commentaries will fall into this stylistic pattern in exactly the same way. In order that you can begin to find out for yourself, here are extracts from other commentaries for analysis and discussion.

7.2.2 Trooping the Colour (radio commentary)

Part of a full commentary of the ceremony is transcribed and set out below, showing initial linking words in one column, separately from the main text.

Adverbs like *then* and *now* do not have to come first. Their **unmarked** position is clause-final, that is, at the end. If they do come first, then they are in the **marked** position which we have called **theme**.

marked position: *now* the Queen rides round (*now* is **thematic**)
unmarked position: the Queen rides round *now*

Exercise 1

Listen to the tape-recording (Section 22) and complete the transcription.

Exercise 2

What is the frequency, in this commentary, of (a) thematic adverbials and (b) deletion? Explain the reasons for what you discover.

Exercise 3

Compare the prosodic features of the commentator's speech - intonation (pitch, loudness, tempo) and stress with those of the football commentator.

(1) now   the royal procession having completed the
                                   inspection

	the Queen rides back towards us here to the saluting base
	led by the Brigade-Major and those four brilliant Life Guards
(2)	the Queen somehow looking regal graceful and military all at the same time
(3)	the next order will be the one word 'Troop' from Colonel Golson
not perhaps	the most difficult of the one hundred and thirteen words of command believe it or not which he has to remember
(4) but	it sets off a whole chain of events including the actual Trooping itself
(5) first	the massed bands of all five Guards regiments march and counter-march in slow and quick time
	three hundred and eighty of the finest military musicians in the world
	nineteen ranks of twenty
	a stunning square down there to the left of musical military skill
	formidable in size sound experience and showmanship
(6) at their heads	five drum-majors
	coats of gold lace
	gold maces in their hands

7.2.3 Snooker match

The following short extract from the commentary on a televised snooker match suggests that deletion does not depend upon the speed and excitement of an event. Snooker is not a fast game, and there are lengthy periods of silence in the commentary.

Here is a transcription of the commentary on the last few minutes of a frame.

Exercise

(a) Identify the places of deleted elements and suggest words to fill them in.

(b) Comment on any difficulties which the vocabulary might present to anyone knowing nothing about the game of snooker.

(c) Discuss possible reasons why the commentator does not use complete sentences, although he has plenty of time.

(*1*) and obviously Steve can't squeeze between the brown and the blue (0.1) so just looking to try and possibly come off the side cushion (.) and rest against this red on the back cushion
(0.24)
(*2*) no it looks as though he's coming round the angles very (*unfinished*) (0.6) I think he was trying to snick off one of those two reds and go back to baulk but a very risky shot to play and he's been rather fortunate the white has finished up tight on the cushion
(0.7)
(*3*) eleven points in it then
(0.55)
(*4*) can cut this red into the right-hand centre pocket (.) just put a little screw on the white ball to hold it for the black and just needs good position on the black to clinch this game
(0.50)
(*5*) and that's a good one (0.2) yes just the black and the last red to leave Steve needing snookers

7.3 Conversation

Ordinary conversation is perhaps the most important variety of social language use, and the most basic, in the sense that in infancy we learn language in order to interact with other people, and we continue to converse daily with others throughout our lives. **Conversational analysis** has become an important branch of language study, and is trying to discover more exactly just what the rules of ordinary conversation are.

For example, one of the basic skills is that of **turn-taking** (cf. chapter 6). How do you *know* when to take your turn in conversation? Why is it that in most normal conversation there is hardly any **overlap** of speakers?

What are the functions of pauses and silence? How do you 'repair' a part of a conversation that has broken down through misunderstanding or mishearing? How do you recognise a **request** when you hear one?

The two conversations examined in chapter 5, where the differences between speech and writing were discussed, are not typical of what we think of as normal everyday conversation. They were specially set up and recorded, and the father took on a directing role, asking questions and generally keeping the talk going. To get really spontaneous conversation, the speakers need to be quite uninhibited and unaware of the tape-recorder. The problem of how to record genuine conversation has been called 'the observer's paradox':

> . . .the aim of linguistic research in the community must be to find out how people talk when they are not being systematically observed; yet we can only obtain this data by systematic observation. (William Labov, 'The study of language in its social context', *Studium Generale*, 23, 1970)

To record a conversation when speakers are unaware is not acceptable, so you should always obtain permission to record someone's speech. Even if you do, a satisfactory recording of conversation, for purposes of study, is difficult to achieve. A BBC television series in the 1970s successfully overcame the observer's paradox by filming and recording a working-class family's daily activities over a long period, with the cameras and microphones set up in their home and following them around wherever they went. The members of the family became so used to the presence of cameras that they produced what appeared to be completely normal behaviour and speech – so normal that some viewers objected to the language used from time to time.

The three following extracts from the series show examples of dialogue in different situations, and illustrate how we adapt our behaviour and use of English to fit the context. (Cassette tape Sections 23-25).

Exercise

(a) Examine the ways in which the speakers signal their meanings, moods and intentions, and listen particularly to:

(i) **voice quality**:
pitch – is it relatively high or low?
pitch movement – does it rise or fall, or is there a combination of rise and fall?
stress – is there any contrastive or emphatic stress?
loudness – is the speech soft or loud, increasing or decreasing in loudness?
tempo – is the speed of delivery faster or slower than normal?

(ii) **turn-taking**:(cf. chapter 6)
what clues are there in one person's speech which allow the other speaker to take a turn?

is there any overlapping, if so, is it deliberate or accidental, and why?

what means does a speaker use to 'hold the floor' and prevent the other from taking a turn?

(iii) **pauses**:
do different lengths or placing of pauses have different meanings in the interaction?

(b) Relate these features to the speakers' intentions in each of the dialogues.

(c) Discuss the speakers' regional dialect and accent.

(The symbols == show where one speaker 'latches' onto another without a break)

1. Tom B. and Mrs W. (Cassette tape Section 23)

(Tom has been living with W.'s daughter Marion, and Mrs W. asks him when he intends to get married.)

TB. everybody else has been talking about marriage (1.0) but I'm the
one that's getting married (.) we will get married like you
know (.) we intend (.) to get married and that but not just yet   5
MW. don't get me wrong I'm not interfering I//just want to know what
TB.   oh no oh no
MW. you think about why you don't want to get married I mean
you're both over eighteen nothing I can do but I don't like
seeing Marion hurt   10
TB. I don't want to get married just yet li.like you know (1.0) and I
think myself//. . .
MW.   well I think you'd find (.) she// wants to be
TB.   mm
MW. married before she moves into that flat   15
TB. oh I think *she* does yeah
MW. well don't you consider her at all I mean
(1.0)
TB. oh yeah but I don't want to get married just yet (2.0) you see=
MW. =well but what do you call just yet? [*laughs*]   20
TB. I mean a few more months at least I mean I'm not going to rush
into marriage in seven weeks' time (1.0) it's as simple as that
(.) I mean mea. Mar. Marion either takes it or she leaves it (.)
I'm not getting married // just yet
MW.   what if she leaves it?   25
TB. well it's (1.0) that's it then isn't it?

2. *Heather and Mrs W.* (Cassette tape Section 24)

(The mother and daughter are talking about a married sister, Karen, who had been living in the house with her husband and child, and who has now moved into her own flat.)

H.   the first day she moved out she had to come round here
      (6.0)

MW.   your father and I were talking this morning (.) and we said that
      when you (.) get married (.) and have a home of your own (2.0)
      you're going to be nice and strong (.) you'll be able to cope on   5
      your own //(.) you'll keep the place really spotless and you'll

H.   I will (.) I will (.) I'll make my friends

MW.   make friends (.) well we said all this because you're a very
      strong character

H.   all right=   10

MW.   =now listen

H.   but Mum what what would she do if none of us lived around here or
      if she had to get a house out of Reading what would she do?
      // you tell me that

MW.   she would have (.) she would have to manage   15

H.   exactly (.) so why don't she // start trying to now? // but no

MW.   yes   but the

H.   she can't because you seem to try to let her (.)

MW.   point is she's not such a strong character=

H.   =it's not the point she's as str. she's stronger than what she   20
      makes out I'll tell you now

MW.   well maybe

H.   she's a lot stronger cos otherwise I would have drived her mad
      when she lived here but no she's a lot stronger than what she
      makes out to you lot I'll tell you that now   25

MW.   well I'm just trying to help her get // (.) acclimatised

H.   yeah

MW.   // so therefore I try to do it gradually

H.   exactly you helped her (.) you helped her when she come here
      you helped her when she come here (.) then you had to help her in   30
      doing other things when she was here (.) then you helped her in
      summat else then summat else then summat else (.) now she's gone
      you're helping her in summat else again // and then it'll be

MW.   well I'm just

H.   summat else and summat else and summat else (1.0) but in the long 35
      run you ain't going to help her because she's going to be lost
      (1.0)

MW. well then I've then I've done all I can haven't I? // I have the
H.   exactly (.)
MW. satisfaction of knowing I've tried   40
H.   now you needn't bother any more (.) you have tried (.) you've
     tried more than anyone // has tried (.) and now you've got to
MW.   right (.) so now I'm gradually trying
H.   give up
MW. to break her off coming up so often   45
H.   exactly (.) because you might as well just give up
MW. well why and why should I give up?
H.   because (.) you ain't // helping her no more
MW.   did I give up on you?
H.   don't bother I don't need your help though   50
     (1.0)
MW. as I say // it's nice to have people there
H.   that's the trouble with you lot you're too soft on her
     (1.0)
     the more you lot are like that the worse she's going to be   55
     (2.0) it's Karen all over if she know she got it coming cushy she
     ain't got to bother have she?

3. Tom, Marion, and the Minister (Cassette tape, Section 25)
(Tom has at last agreed on a wedding date, and he and Marion go to
the minister of the church where they want to be married.)

(a) First extract
Mi. I've been watching (.) you know the // (.) programme // on TV
Ma.   [laughs]
T.   the programme
Mi. (.) I'm not preaching at you (.) but as a minister of // this
T.   mm   mm   5
Mi. church that em (.) I naturally (.) stand for the Christian
     doctrine of marriage // (1.0) and er (.) you are sincere in that
T.   mm
Mi. you want to (.) marry (.) Marion // (.) and really make a go of
T.   mm yeah   10
Mi. it (.) that is so // isn't it?
T.   oh
T.   oh that is so (.) yeah (.) well I mean we definitely do intend

	to (.) make a go of it and that // (.) I mean (.) we had (.)	
Mi.	yes good	15
T.	we've been intending to get married for a long (.) quite a while now like // you know	
Mi.	that's right yes (.) you'll remember for many a day (.) the vows that you've made to each other (.) because although it's a simple service it's a profound service	20
T.	mm	
Ma.	mm	

(b) Second extract

Mi.	had you thought of the organ? er // (.) had you looked that far	
Ma.	em	
Mi.	ahead yet?=	
Ma.	=not really actually I've // em	
Mi.	oh (1.0) normally these days we	5
	don't sing 'The Voice that Breath'd o'er Eden' // (1.0) er you	
T.	[laughs]	
Ma.	[laughs]	
Mi.	know (.) neither do we sing 'Rescue the Perishing'	
T.	I was just about to say yes that you would really want one	10
	because as you say it sort of puts the finishing touches to it	
	// sort of thing	
Mi.	that's right // (.) yes	
Ma.	well you'd (.) it'd be dead without it wouldn't	
	it? // (.) mm	15
Mi.	yes yes good (2.0) now is there any question you'd like to	
	(.) bring to me?	
	(1.0)	
T.	see when we f. first we thought you know er me and Marion started	
	living together and that // (.) we thought that might have had	20
Mi.	mm	
T.	the effect on the Church like you know (.) I mean	
Mi.	look Tom (.) if only people would remember (.) we're not here to	
	(.) prejudge anybody // (.) I'm not // (.) and I (.) I say	
T.	mm yeah	25
Mi.	this(.) that if I can perform this service // (.) to get you to	
T.	mm	
Mi.	do the (1.0) honour//able thing you know // (.) then you can face	
T.	honourable thing which is marriage	

Mi.   the world // (.) and you say (.) she belongs to me // (.) I
T.   mm   mm
Mi.   belong // to her (.) it's as simple as that
T.   mm

8

Variety and style in written English — I. Reporting the news

8.1 What the headlines say

Newspaper headlines have a familiar and conventional linguistic structure not unlike telegrams in their brevity. Here we shall discuss their function in press reports, and in particular how they present the ideology of the newspaper. By *ideology* is meant the system of beliefs about society which underlie the reporting of news.

The wording of a headline is affected by at least three things: (i) the ideas to be expressed, (ii) the technology of printing, and (iii) the kind of reader associated with a particular paper. We expect a different selection of news items and kinds of photograph in the tabloid papers, compared with the broadsheets, as well as differences of typography and style. These differences will be expressed in the headlines also.

A newspaper editor's description of the function of headlines, and how they should be written, is presented in the book *News Headlines*, which is part of the series *Editing and Design*, by Harold Evans. The series was written as a training manual for journalists.

Harold Evans' three criteria for good headline writing are simplicity, informality, and impact. The headline, he says, should be a clear signal, swiftly readable, economical in reading time and space, and its style in proportion to the news it reports. In other words, there is a test of acceptability relevant to good headline English as well as to other styles of writing.

Exercise 1

(a) Collect a series of headlines from two or more different daily newspapers, and evaluate them according to the three criteria of simplicity, informality, and impact.

(b)   Are there differences between the headline styles of tabloid and broadsheet newspapers?

(c)   What are the linguistic features of headlines by which you identify the three criteria?

Exercise 2

Read these three quotations from *News Headlines*, and answer the questions which follow:

(i)   'A single consistent style emphasises the journalistic effort of the newspaper to produce some semblance of comprehensible order from the disordered world.'

(ii)   'The headline must tell the news. Many who do not read the story none the less retain an impression from scanning the headlines.'

(iii) 'All good headlines follow certain rules, in what they say and how they say it. What they say is the single most urgent newspoint, as the newspaper sees it, accurately, intelligibly, and impartially. Accuracy and impartiality are the most important basic constituents'.

(a)   What does Harold Evans mean by his opposition of *order* in the newspaper and *disorder* in the world?

(b)   Scan the headlines of two different newspapers and consider what impressions you get of the worlds they present.

(c)   Harold Evans condemns 'selective perception' and 'the odious practice of using loaded words'. If it is the job of a newspaper to *interpret* and *explain* the news, as well as to report it, is it in fact possible for it to avoid selective perception and be impartial?

   (You should return to this question again after you have finished the chapter.)

Obvious selective perception, or bias, can be seen when a newspaper does not report a particular event which other papers do report, or when certain features of an event are reported and not others. But choices have to be made because space is limited, just as, in radio and television news, time is limited. Compare the selection of items which appear in a two-minute news flash compared with a thirty-minute broadcast, for example. These choices, though important, are not linguistic matters. This study is confined to language use – how the news which *is* chosen for reporting is presented.

The claim of <u>impartiality</u> in news reporting will be tested in this section by closely analysing some headlines, and in section 8.2 by examining extracts from complete reports. We shall show that the vocabulary and grammar of headlines and news reports combine to reveal a distinctive point of view, which implies at least some partiality or bias.

Here are two pairs of headlines, taken from two daily newspapers, reporting the same events.

1.   (A)   FOUR BR COMPANIES TO BE SOLD OFF
    (B)   LOOTERS LET LOOSE ON BRITISH RAIL ASSETS

2.   (Ai)   Imports influx feared as Post Office profits are creamed off
           JOSEPH CUTS OFF PHONE MONOPOLY
    (Aii) HOWELL TO ALLOW FIRMS TO SELL POWER
    (B)   'Power for profit' plan
           TORIES GRAB 2 INDUSTRIES FOR THE CITY

Exercise 3

Examine the vocabulary and structure of the headlines and assess the views and sympathies of paper (A) and paper (B). (The papers are labelled (A) and (B), because if they were named, your judgement might be affected by your knowledge of the paper's political views, rather than by the linguistic evidence.)

Discuss them, or make your own assessment, before going on to read the analytical commentary.

Commentary

1.   (A)   FOUR BR COMPANIES TO BE SOLD OFF

This appears at first to be impartial, a plain statement of an intended course of action. It is a **passive clause**, and the <u>agent</u> is not included, that is, the person or institution by whom the companies are to be sold off.

But the *Concise Oxford Dictionary* defines *to sell off* as *to clear out stock at reduced prices*, which is not the same as *to sell*. There is therefore an implied attitude of disapproval in (A)'s use of *to sell off*.

(B)   LOOTERS LET LOOSE ON BRITISH RAIL ASSETS

The primary meaning of *to loot* is *to plunder in time of war or civil disorder*. It implies force, and possessions taken illegally.

To let loose is a verb applied to releasing or unchaining, typically a hunting-dog or pack, and has **connotative** or **associative meanings** suggesting fierceness, wildness, an attack on a prey.

Assets means *property which has value*, and which could be used to meet debts, for example.

The obviously unfavourable **connotations** or **associations** of this headline are focused on those institutions, companies, and individuals who might buy British Rail assets if they were given the opportunity. By likening them to looters preying on BR, the headline questions the morality of the proposal.

2.   (Ai) Imports influx feared as Post Office profits are creamed off
       JOSEPH CUTS OFF PHONE MONOPOLY

This is a combination of main headline and overline (or strapline). The overline is an additional explanatory comment on the main headline.

Sir Keith Joseph was the Conservative Secretary for Industry. The use of surname only is usual in headlines, although in a text it would contrast in formality and politeness with *Sir Keith*, or the full name with title.

The use of *cuts off*, a term from the vocabulary of the telephone industry in relation to customers who don't pay their bills, is obviously deliberate. (Some newspapers are known for their use of punning in headlines and news reports.) The headline refers to *monopoly* – the exclusive possession of the right to trade in some commodity – but does not seem to approve or disapprove, and so appears impartial.

But the overline is more explicit. *To cream off* is to take away the richest part, and here may indicate disapproval which the text of the report might confirm or not.

(Aii)   HOWELL TO ALLOW FIRMS TO SELL POWER

Mr David Howell was Secretary for Energy. The government's policy included the privatisation of the whole or parts of previously nationalised industries. This headline refers to proposals which would allow private companies to generate and sell electricity, and appears neutral in its attitude.

(B)   'Power for profit' plan
TORIES GRAB 2 INDUSTRIES FOR THE CITY

One headline with overline in (B) covers both proposals. The word *profit* will carry connotations of either approval or disapproval in relation to trade and industry, depending on the point of view of the speaker/writer and of the listener/reader, and whether they consider the making of private profit an acceptable activity or not.

The word *Tory* goes back to the later seventeenth century, and like other terms which were originally impolite, has now become acceptable for *Conservative* by Conservatives. But it retains connotations of disapproval when used by non-Conservatives. (Compare the use of the word *Socialist* in some newspapers when referring to the Labour party.)

So the connotative meanings of words are relative to the speaker and listener, and slight differences may carry significant overtones of meaning. The same words can be either favourable or unfavourable in their meanings, depending upon who is writing and reading them.

The main headline in 2(B) is markedly loaded against the government's proposals:

grab: *to seize suddenly*, *snatch at*, implying selfish motives and impolite actions.

the City: *the City of London*, the phrase representing the international financial centre made up of the banks and companies whose main offices and work are in the City of London.

for the City implies that the government is making proposals for selling nationalised industries on behalf of, for the profit of, traders in the City, and not for disinterested motives.

The language of 1(B) and 2(B) implies a model of society different from that of paper (A).

Exercise 4

Discuss the connotative meanings, for different speakers and listeners, of:

Communist, Red, Conservative, comrade, Fascist, extremist, reactionary, solidarity, democratic, Left-wing, Right-wing, bully-boy, capitalist, law and order.

Exercise 5

Take a report on the same event from two newspapers, preferably of opposing views, and find words and phrases with marked contrasting connotative meanings.

Exercise 6

Examine the differences in the reporting of news in the following pairs of headlines, from the same newspapers (A) and (B). They describe a series of events at a British Leyland factory. Industrial strikes are staple items of news, but disputes at British Leyland were at one time given specially extensive coverage. Sir Michael Edwardes was chairman of BL.

EVENTS AT BRITISH LEYLAND

(i)   (A)   Company decides to put its case directly to workers
            STEWARDS CALL FOR ALL-OUT BL STRIKE
      (B)   Stewards reject final offer
            EDWARDES' BID TO BREAK BL STRIKE VOTE
(ii) (A)   EDWARDES TELLS BL UNIONS THAT STRIKE WOULD BRING
            CLOSURE
      (B)   LEYLAND AT CRUNCH AS PAY TALKS FAIL
(iii) (A)   BL UNIONS END STRIKE THREAT AS 1,600 JOBS ARE LOST
            AT TALBOT
      (B)   DON'T MISTAKE OUR ANGER, SAYS LEYLAND CONVENOR
(iv) (A)   Police at Longbridge as anger mounts over 500 lay offs
            TROUBLE FLARES AS BL WORKERS DEMONSTRATE
      (B)   METRO FURY AS WORKERS LAID OFF AT DROP OF HAT

Commentary

(i) Both (A) and (B) have headlines with overlines, but the content of (A)'s headline is in (B)'s overline, and vice versa. This shows an interesting contrast in the assessment of the major item of news.

(A)   Company decides to put its case directly to workers
       STEWARDS CALL FOR ALL-OUT BL STRIKE

The union shop stewards in the BL factory are the **initiators** of the action of *calling a strike*. In grammatical terms, *stewards* is the **subject** of the clause and also its **theme**, coming first.

Since shop stewards are the intermediaries between the company and the workers, there are obvious implications in the use of *directly* in the overline. The stewards are to be by-passed and normal procedures not followed.

Notice the identification of three **participants** in the **verbal processes** of *calling for* and *deciding to put a case to*:
(a) the company, (b) the stewards, and (c) the workers.

(B)   Stewards reject final offer
       EDWARDES' BID TO BREAK BL STRIKE VOTE

The chairman of BL is here the **initiator** of the action, or the attempted action, *bid*. The strike has not yet taken place, but a vote in favour of a strike has been obtained. To *break a strike* is to use some kind of force to end it, so that the the strikers are unsuccessful.

The word *break* has strong historical associations for trade unionists, linked with past actions by governments and employers in using the police and the armed forces as *strike-breakers*. To use it in relation to a *vote* is to evoke these associations of violent confrontaion.

The overline implies the participation of BL management, even though the phrase *by the company* does not appear. The offer, we infer, was not good enough. Notice that *stewards* is the subject and thus the theme of the headline, so the stewards are presented as the initiators of the action, and focus of interest.

(ii)   (A)   EDWARDES TELLS BL UNIONS THAT STRIKE WOULD BRING
CLOSURE

A few days later, and the company has put its case directly to the workers.

The chairman is the iniator, but again of a verbal process, *tells*. To some extent, the headline dissociates him from responsibility for the results of a strike. The **modal auxiliary verb** *would*, like other modals in English, is ambiguously vague.

In *strike would bring closure*, *closure*, the **object** of *bring* (= *cause*), is presented as a direct result of *strike*, the **subject** of the clause, so that it is the strikers who are said to initiate the action of causing the closure of the company. But only the chairman and board of directors of a company have power to close it, so the headline omits the essential fact of the chairman's responsibility.

The modal verb *would* has a 'softening' effect on the underlying implications of what is really a *threat*. One of its meanings suggests 'possibility' only. But what the chairman meant was almost certainly: EDWARDES WILL CLOSE BL IF WORKERS STRIKE. What does this suggest about the newspaper's attitude?

Notice also how the grammar of the newspaper headline uses nouns, not verbs, for actions. In fact, it is people who strike, and close things. Turning an action into a 'thing', using nouns for verbs, is called **nominalisation**, and is an often-used device which allows you to avoid implying that individual men and women are directly responsible for causing things to happen.

The version 'Edwardes will close BL if workers strike' replaces the nouns of the original headline (*strike* and *closure*) with verbs (*strike* and *close* - the word *strike* can be a noun or a verb). 'Strike would bring closure' relieves the chairman of any blame.

(B)   LEYLAND AT CRUNCH AS PAY TALKS FAIL

The colloquial *at crunch* implies a decisive event which is imminent, but the headline itself does not make clear what the event - whether to strike or not - might be. The *as*-clause suggests both time (*when*) and reason (*because*). The noun *talks* is the subject of the verb *fail*, but this is shorthand for 'management and unions fail to agree'. This paper does not headline Sir Michael Edwardes' statement/ threat.

(iii)   (A)   BL UNIONS END STRIKE THREAT AS 1,600 JOBS ARE LOST
              AT TALBOT

The strike did not happen, and a majority of the workers in BL
voted to accept the pay offer of the management. The representatives
who were negotiating (the unions) had to accept this vote, and are
reported as initiating the action which ended the threat.

The loss of jobs in another car manufacturing firm's factory is head-
lined as a significant event in relation to BL: 'as 1,600 jobs are lost at
Talbot' is a subordinate clause and implies both cause and simultaneous
action. (Subordinate clauses in headlines are rare, but when they do
occur, they are almost always *as*-clauses.)

(B)   DON'T MISTAKE OUR ANGER, SAYS LEYLAND CONVENOR

A reader must know several things to understand this headline: (a)
knowledge of the series of events conveyed by the one word *Leyland*,
and (b) of the structure of trade unions, and the role of a convenor – a
senior official who convenes meetings of the shop stewards – and (c)
knowledge that the strike is already off, so that the anger of the convenor can be understood as directed against the manner in which the
settlement was reached.

Paper (B), in headlining the fact that the strike was not amicably
settled, is supporting the convenor's point of view.

(iv)   (A)   Police at Longbridge as anger mounts over 500 lay offs
             TROUBLE FLARES AS BL WORKERS DEMONSTRATE

Overline and main headline combine to cover several aspects of events
which occurred only a few weeks later.

The subject and theme of the first part of the overline is *Police*. The
use of the police is considered to be of primary importance. The reason
is implied in the *as*-clause, with the attribution of anger as a result of
(*over)* 500 workers being laid off.

The police are not called in because people are angry, however, but
because they are acting in a way which is interpreted as being in breach
of the law, like a disturbance of the peace, or damage to persons and
property. So the headlining of the use of the police has important
implications.

Trouble flares is similar in its meaning to *anger mounts*, a stage later, the effects of a cause.

To demonstrate is used as an **intransitive verb**, meaning *to make a public protest*. A public demonstration is legal, but the headline implies a series of events, with cause and effect inferred by the reader from the word order. In conveying information, the first word or phrase in a clause (the theme), and the last (where new information tends to be put), are important. So if we take the first and last words in the overline and headline, and rearrange them in their chronological order, we get:

lay-offs – demonstrate – trouble – police

or, 'the managers laid off a number of workers who then demonstrated and caused trouble which led to someone calling in the police'.

This summarises paper (A)'s interpretation of the events. But it is the *police* and *trouble* which are made the most prominent as the themes of the overline and headline, not the *lay-offs* and the *demonstration*. Whose side does the paper take, whether intentionally or not?

(B)   METRO FURY AS WORKERS LAID OFF AT DROP OF HAT

(B)'s headline includes (A)'s *anger* as *fury*, which is somewhat stronger, but does not mention *police*, *demonstration*, or *trouble*. It adds the information that the workers were engaged on production of the Metro car, and comments adversely against management, by implication, in the colloquial phrase *at (the) drop of (a) hat*.

These analyses and commentaries do not imply that all headlines can be dissected for clear evidence of point of view or bias. But examining headlines from two or more papers will sometimes reveal conflicting interpretations of events. Consistent interpretations within each paper make up their contrasting ideologies.

Exercise 7

Analyse the following groups of headlines, which report the same items of news in the two newspapers from which the preceding examples have been taken.

(i)
- **(A)** Civil Service unions likely to protest at attempt to limit pay
  6 pc LIMIT STAYS BUT MPs WIN BIG RISE
- **(B)** Unions see red at rise for Soames
  £27,825 FOR ME, PEANUTS FOR YOU

(ii)
- **(A)** £500m PACKAGE AIMED AT CUTTING JOBLESS BY 216,000
  MEASURES A BOOST TO TORY MORALE
  GOVERNMENT PACKAGE TO HELP YOUNGSTERS
- **(B)** One year on low pay then sack
  THATCHER PEANUTS PLAN FOR YOUTH
  Hypocrisy and blackmail
- **(C)** (*a third newspaper*)
  First aid for jobless
  MAGGIE'S £700M BOOST FOR JOBS

8.2   News reporting

8.2.1   Style

The style of newspaper reporting in the nineteenth century was very formal in both vocabulary and grammar. This tradition still holds to some extent for the 'quality' newspapers today, but they themselves were affected by the changes in size, layout, and style brought about by the popular newspapers in 'tabloid' form. Too often, people condemn the popularisation of daily newspapers without bothering to assess the good and bad in them. An interesting commentary on tabloid style is contained in *Daily Mirror Style* by Keith Waterhouse.

He describes good popular newspaper style in this way:

> It is a plain, straightforward, well-ordered narrative, completely without gimmicks. There are no fancy words, and no needless words. . . .The material is arranged chronologically, with the briefest of introductions. No attempt is made to tempt the reader with window-dressing or with lurid shock-drama labels. . . .

These criteria apply both to serious writing about serious matters and to the reporting of ephemeral news in a light mood.

Exercise 1

Here is a short, typical example of a very minor piece of news, to be forgotten almost as soon as read. What are the features of its style that make it clearly a piece of popular reporting?

> SUMMER SPOONFUL 'RIP-OFF'
> Tennis fans were charged £1 for half a dozen strawberries with cream at Wimbledon yesterday.
>
> But at 16p a mouthful, many fans boycotted them. 5
>
> Seasoned Wimbledon-goer Kay Demetriou, 17, took her own punnet of 20 strawberries bought for 28p at a green-grocers up the road. 10
>
> Said Kay, from Streatham, South London: 'I've been ripped off here before.
>
> 'I decided it wasn't going to happen this year.' 15

Commentary

The layout, adopted by all the tabloid newspapers, is one sentence to each paragraph, occasionally two, so that each successive topic is presented very economically.

Sentence structure is also simple, with little use of subordination except a **qualifying clause** (*bought for . . .*) and **quoted clauses** following *said*.

Marked grammatical features lie within the clause. In sentence 2, the adverbial *at 16p a mouthful* comes first as theme, after *but*, which links it to sentence 1.

Seasoned Wimbledon-goer Kay Demetrious, 17, is a compressed noun phrase, with descriptive **pre-modifiers** before the name, and the figure for her age in **apposition** to it.

Notice the inversion of *Said Kay*, and the descriptive **post-modifier** following it.

Vocabulary is informal, sometimes colloquial, e.g. *rip-off*.

Exercise 2

Make your own commentary on the following news report, describing the marked features of the language which are typical of popular journalistic style.

M-WAY SHOCK BY WHIZZKID

Drivers on a motorway were startled by the machine whizzing along with them.

For six-year-old Robert Flynn decided to take his diddy BMX bike on the M57 near Wolverhampton for a test run. And with legs moving like pistons, he tried to keep up with the traffic.

Stunned

Driving in the opposite direction was quick-thinking Dave Hodgetts, who shot off the motorway at the next junction and zoomed back to overtake Robert.

'I was stunned,' said Dave, of Brookside, Telford, Shrops. 'The lad's little legs were racing away and he looked really determined.'

Dave stopped Robert and called the police because he was worried about the risk of an accident.

Soon afterwards a real speed machine drew up – a police Jaguar. And Robert was treated to a ride home to Hedgerow Walk, Wolverhampton.

He was let off with a lecture – and warned not to ride too fast.

8.2.2   Ideology and bias

We now return to the major topic of this chapter, already introduced in the discussion of headlines – the question of impartiality and selective perception in news reporting.

Exercise 3

(a)   Read the two reports printed below, 'Sheffield incident' (pp. 168-9).
(b)   By reading the headlines only, what impression of the incident do you obtain from each paper?

Exercise 4

Look for answers to these questions in each report:
(a)   Identify the 'single most urgent news point, as the paper sees it' and give the evidence for your conclusion.
(b)   Look at the connotations of important lexical items. For example, what is the effect, on your perception of the events, of the italicised words or phrases in the following extracts? Try substituting alternative words, and assess the difference:

1.   big Thatcher *nosh* – (A): headline;
2.   The People's March for Jobs '83 banner *stood proud* – (A), para. 4;
3.   the banners which *festooned* the forecourt – (A), para. 5;
4.   the evening went *peacefully* – (A), para. 6;
5.   the *drama* happened – (B), para. 3;
6.   the Prime Minister *braved* 3,000 protestors – (B); para. 3;
7.   speakers. . .*tried to speak* to the crowd – (B); para. 11;
8.   *missiles* were thrown – (B), para. 9.

Can you find any other words which have definite connotations?

Exercise 5

Rewriting the text in certain ways can be helpful, for example, setting out the actions of each participant separately. This reveals both how the participants are named and what they are said to have done.

What is the important difference between the two reports shown by the following rewriting of the actions of the police horse?

(The sign ∅ indicates a participant reference which has been grammatically deleted from the text.)

participant	action	
(A)		
a police horse	bolted	into the police car
the horse	fell	over the boot of the car
∅	breaking	the rear window
= *3 references*		
(B)		
a police horse	bolted	
it	threw	its woman rider
∅	crashed	into. . .a police car
(its face)	smashing	a window
her mount	frightened	(by a missile)
the animal	bolted	past a line of police
he	tried to get round	the. . .car
he	slipped	
∅	unseated	WPC Wilson
∅	snapped	his bridle
the horse	smashed into	the back of the Jaguar
∅	dashing off	
= *12 references*		

Exercise 6

Write out similar analyses for (a) the rider, (b) the police, (c) the diners, (d) Mrs Thatcher, and then comment on the significant differences you find between them.

Exercise 7

Perhaps the most important contrast between the two reports lies in their interpretation of the crowd's behaviour. Use the following summary to comment on each paper's attitude towards the composition of the crowd and its behaviour.

(A)		
5,000 people	demonstrated	(colourfully)
	opposed	Mrs Thatcher's policies

	packed	the forecourt of the Cathedral
	stood	for one minute's silence
	booed & hissed	the diners
	(brought)	banners
	played music	

(B)

3,000 protestors	demonstrated	(noisily)
	protested	
	threw	eggs & flour
	aimed	missile at WPC
	caused trouble	for WPC
	made noise	
	threw	missiles
	drowned out	speeches of their own speakers
	shouted	'Maggie out'

The people/protestors are named as follows:

(A)   *people of Sheffield*: the Sheffield unemployed, trade unionists, peace activists and Asian people
trade unions and local groups: NUR, TGWU, NUPE, Bangladeshi community, Asian youth movement, Sheffield street band, Caribbean group

(B)   crowd of trade unionists and city council leaders like NUM President Arthur Scargill and city council leader David Blunkett
supporters; crowd

Exercise 8

Now make a summary of the principal differences between the two newspaper reports, using the *selection of events* in each paper, and the *language used* to describe each selection as the basis of your commentary.

(1)   SHEFFIELD INCIDENT
(The paragraphs are numbered for easy reference.)

Report (A)

BOOS FOR BIG THATCHER NOSH

1. In a colourful demonstration, the people of Sheffield showed Mrs Thatcher the strength of the opposition to her policies last night as she arrived at the Master Cutlers' annual feast.

2. About 5,000 people packed the forecourt of the Sheffield Cathedral opposite the Cutlers' Hall from 5.30 until 7.30 when they stood for one minute's silence for the millions unemployed.

3. As the diners arrived by luxury coach bejewelled and in formal evening wear, the Sheffield unemployed, trade unionists, peace activists, and Asian people, booed and hissed.

4. The People's March for Jobs '83 banner stood proud in the centre of the sea of banners from trade unions and local groups.

5. Among the banners which festooned the forecourt were those from the Sheffield NUR, TGWU, NUPE, South Yorkshire ASTMS, NALGO, Sheffield Peace Movement, the Sheffield Bangladeshi community and the Asian youth movement.

6. Over a thousand police were brought on to protect Thatcher from the crowds, but the evening went peacefully with music from the celebrated Sheffield Street Band and a Caribbean group.

7. Earlier, a police horse bolted into a police car heading the Premier's cavalcade. The rider slid off as the horse fell over the boot of the car, breaking the rear window.

Report (B)

POLICE HORSE BOLTS IN BIG MAGGIE DEMO

1.   A police horse bolted at the height of a noisy demonstration against Mrs Thatcher last night.

2.   It threw its woman rider and crashed into the rear of a police car, its face smashing a window.

3.   The drama happened as the Prime Minister braved 3,000 protestors to attend the Annual Cutlers' Feast in Sheffield.

4.   As she stepped from her black Jaguar, eggs, flour and apples were thrown from the crowd of trade unionists and city council leaders.

5.   But one missile, aimed near Jane Wilson, South Yorkshire Police's only woman horse rider, frightened her mount, a five-year-old gelding called Fusilier. The animal bolted past a line of police and Press.

6.   As he tried to get round the back of Mrs Thatcher's car, he slipped, unseated WPC Wilson and snapped his bridle.

Missiles

7.   The horse smashed into the back of the Jaguar before dashing off down the road with helmeted WPC Wilson chasing.

8.   A senior officer said: 'Jane was obviously having trouble before the Prime Minister arrived because of the crowd.

9.   'She was doing her best under difficult circumstances but as the Prime Minister arrived the crowd's noise reached a crescendo and missiles were thrown.'

10.   Mrs Thatcher was hustled inside the Cutlers Hall and did not see the incident 25 feet away.

11.   The city council had provided scaffolding for a stage where speakers like NUM President Arthur Scargill and city council leader David Blunkett tried to speak to the crowd, almost outnumbered by police.

12.   Speeches were drowned out by their own supporters with shouts of 'Maggie out.'

13.   Police said 13 people had been arrested, including a juvenile and a girl. Two were for assault, three for throwing eggs and the rest for breach of the peace.

Commentary

The two reports are contrasted in several ways. (A) headlines the crowd response and refers disparagingly to the event which the Prime Minister was attending by using the colloquial word *nosh* for *feast*. Of seven paragraphs, only the last reports the bolting of a police horse.

The bolting of the horse is not only the topic of the headline of (B), but also the subject of seven of the thirteen paragraphs.

If you have made a close study of the text in the way suggested, you will probably agree that paper (A) describes the whole event as primarily a peaceful and colourful anti-government demonstration, and contrasts the situation of the unemployed with that of those attending the feast by implication.

Paper (B) describes the demonstration as a noisy and potentially violent occasion by concentrating upon the personal drama of the police horse and woman rider. There are also inconsistencies in (B)'s text.

In describing an event which it defines as news, a newspaper's choice of vocabulary and grammatical structures will give evidence of attitudes to participants and actions which are not impartial – in other words, there is selective perception.

Two reports of an incident which took place during and after a funeral in Belfast, Northern Ireland offer interesting differences.

Exercise 9

Assess the point of view of each report from a first reading.

(2)   BELFAST INCIDENT

Report (A)

ARMY SWOOP ON FUNERAL RIFLEMEN

1.   Savage street fighting broke out in Republican West Belfast yesterday after an Army snatch squad moved in to arrest and disarm three uniformed and masked Provisional IRA men minutes after they had fired a volley of shots over the coffin of Joseph McDonnell, the Maze hunger striker who died on Wednesday after 61 days without food.

2.   At least four men and a woman were arrested. A number of rifles were recovered.

3.   The three armed men, acting under orders from a Gaelic-speaking officer, emerged from the crowd as the huge funeral procession made its way down the Falls Road towards the Mill Town cemetery.

4.   They aimed the volley over the tricolour draped coffin of Mr McDonnell which was flanked on either side by other IRA men in masks and uniforms.

5.   On orders from the officer, they fired the volley and attempted to disappear, aided by other mourners who held out opened umbrellas to hide them from photographers and television crews.

6.   Moving through a funnel which opened up in the crowd, the men made for a house nearby, presumably to change from uniforms into civilian clothing.

7.   At that point, an army squad, backed up by a large number of other soldiers and police who had been hiding behind a row of houses, moved in to attempt to arrest them.

8.   The house the men made for had probably been pinpointed by Army surveillance helicopters, which constantly circled the funeral procession.

9.   Scores of youths broke off from the funeral procession which continued towards the cemetery and made a determined attempt to prevent the soldiers from reaching the house.

10.   At least five pistol or rifle shots were heard, but it is not clear where they came from. As the youths tore up paving stones and bombarded the Army with a fusillade of missiles, the soldiers kept them at bay by firing a constant barrage of rubber bullets.

11.   The police said that when the Army squad broke into the house they were confronted by armed men. Two of the men were shot and one was detained and taken to hospital, where his condition was described last night as serious.

12.   The other gunman, although wounded, escaped. The search for him is continuing. A woman in the house was arrested and in a follow-up operation four other men were also arrested.

13.   In the house the Army found three Garrand rifles, combat jackets, hoods and gloves.

14.   As the battle raged, women and children screamed. Some mothers threw their children on to the ground and lay on top of them. Other people who had been lining the funeral route took sanctuary in a church.

15.   The police denied that the security forces had fired rubber bullets indiscriminately.

Report (B)

TROOPS FIRE PLASTIC BULLETS INTO MOURNERS

1.   British troops fired a hail of plastic bullets into mourners at the massive funeral of Long Kesh hunger striker Joe McDonnell yesterday – and within minutes much of West Belfast was in uproar.

2.   Thousands came for the funeral of the hunger striker, the fifth to die, but after the IRA colour party had fired the now traditional volley of shots over his flag-draped coffin, the troops stormed in.

3.   An army statement later claimed that five of the men involved in the firing party had been captured along with several of the weapons after shots had been fired in a house.

4.   Armoured cars ferried troops into a pitched battle as plastic bullets were replied to with stones.

Exercise 10

Answer the following questions:

(a)   Few people read two daily newspapers. What impression of the incident is likely to be given to readers of each paper from the headlines only?

(b)   Discuss the choice of vocabulary in the following selected paired extracts, and what the choices tell us about the paper's point of view towards the events.

(c)   Find other paired extracts and analyse their differences.

	Paper (A)	Paper (B)
1.	*the soldiers*	*British troops*

What does the use of *British* in (B) imply?

Do you find the use of the word *troops* more, or less favourable than *soldiers*, or do they mean much the same?

2.	*kept them at bay by firing*	*fired*

What are the associative meanings of the phrase *kept them at bay*?

3.	*scores of youths*	*mourners*

If you attend a funeral, you are a mourner, for the time being, whether you are young or old. What is the purpose here of identifying the participants in different ways?

4.	*Joseph McDonnell*	*Joe McDonnell*
	Mr McDonnell	

Joe, a diminutive, is a more informal mode of address than *Joseph* or *Mr*. What is its effect on a reader?

5.	*hunger striker who died on Wednesday after 61 days without food*	*hunger striker, the fifth to die*

Two choices of additional information. Are their implications different?

6.	*three uniformed and masked Provisional IRA men*	*IRA colour party*
	three armed men	*firing party*
	Gaelic-speaking officer	

Contrast the two descriptions, with special reference to the connotations of *uniformed* and *colour/firing party*.

If the officer spoke Gaelic, why did (A) report the fact?

7.	*volley of shots*	*now traditional volley of shots*

Consider the implications of the added *now traditional* in (B).

8.   *paving stones*   *stones*
     a fusillade of missiles
Are the differences important?
9.   *armed men, gunman*   *five of the men*
Would you refer to a soldier as a *gunman*? If not, what does the
word mean?
10. *arrested*   *captured*
What is the significant difference between the two?

Commentary

The two interpretations of the funeral incident are obviously controversial in their difference. It raises the question of the possibility of
neutral reporting. Our choice of language seems to give away our
attitude whether we want it to or not.

(i)   The headlines
Each paper has chosen a different aspect of the sequence of events
to sum up the whole:

ARMY SWOOP ON FUNERAL RIFLEMEN (A)
TROOPS FIRE PLASTIC BULLETS INTO MOURNERS   (B)

Consider firstly the choice of vocabulary.
   Army v. *Troops*; a **collective** noun standing for the official presence
of soldiers in Northern Ireland (*Army*), against a **plural** noun for
soldiers as individuals who perform actions (*troops*).
   swoop on v. *fire plastic bullets*; the first a **metaphor** suggesting the
image of a bird of prey, a sudden attack to seize and carry off; the
second a **literal** statement implying the use of firearms by men.
   funeral riflemen v. *into mourners*; the stated objective of the Army's
plan, *men who fired rifles at a funeral*, contrasts with the object of
attack, *mourners*, in (B)'s headline, which describes a later incident, but
headlines it as the major event.

(ii)   The reports

(a)   Vocabulary: In Exercise 10 you have already examined significant
vocabulary – those words and phrases from both reports which have
more or less the same reference to the events and the participants. The

differences observed in the headlines are consistently found in the reports also.

Notice that the first two paragraphs of (A) are a summary of the principal events of the incident, and some of its items are repeated in the later paragraphs. As a summary, these two paragraphs are directly comparable with the shorter report in (B).

By now you will agree that newspaper (A) is sympathetic to the Army and the task assigned to it in Northern Ireland by the Government, and that (B) is sympathetic towards the IRA.

(b)   Grammatical structure; active and passive clauses: When we describe actions and events, we perceive something going on which involves one or more participants. For example, in *the three armed men. . . attempted to disappear*, the three men, acting as a group, are **actors** performing an **action**. They do the disappearing. The clause might have been simply, *They disappeared*. This kind of clause is called **intransitive**.

Some actions involve two sets of participants, firstly the **actor** who performs it (or the **agent** who causes it to happen), and secondly those who are **affected** by the action. X (the actor/agent) does something to Y (affected). For example,

actor/agent (S)	*action* (P)	*affected* (O)
an army squad	arrest and disarm	three IRA men
British troops	fired	plastic bullets
the youths	bombarded	the Army

These clauses are called **transitive**.

The clause structures relate the actor/agent to the action and the affected person or thing by means of the **word order** represented by SPO – the **subject** is followed by the **predicator**, which is followed by the **object**. Change the order, and the meaning is changed. *The Army arrested three IRA men* does not mean the same as *Three IRA men arrested the Army*.

This SPO structure has the grammatical feature called **active voice**, and can be changed into what is called the **passive voice** very easily. Notice how the actor and the affected participants change places in the clause:

affected (S)		*action* (P)		*actor/agent* (A)
three IRA men	were	arrested and disarmed	by	an Army squad
plastic bullets	were	fired	by	British troops
the Army	was	bombarded	by	the youths

Exercise 11

What are the rules for changing an active clause into a passive clause? Try to answer this from the evidence of the clauses just quoted, but refer to a descriptive grammar also to confirm what you discover.

Now an interesting thing about using the passive form of a transitive clause is that you can leave out the *by*-phrase, which says who the actor/agent was, and the clause remains grammatical. You have omitted some information, of course, but that does not affect the grammatical acceptability of the clause. This can be very useful.

So the clauses could have been written:

Three IRA men were arrested and disarmed.
Plastic bullets were fired.
The Army was bombarded.

The grammatical subject of a clause is important because it comes before the predicator and is usually the theme of the clause also. We may tend to think of the subject of a clause as the actor, even when the clause is passive, because of its prominence.

It is possible, therefore, to imply that the participant who is *affected* by an action (the *object* in an active clause), is actually partly responsible for the action in a passive clause, when it is the subject. This is especially so if the actor/agent in the *by*-phrase in the passive, is omitted.

Exercise 12

(a)   Write down a list of the passive forms actually used in report (A), and answer these questions from your list:

Who arrested the four men and the woman and recovered the rifles?

Who flanked the coffin?
Who aided the IRA men?
Who backed up the Army squad?
Who pinpointed the house?
Who heard the pistol and rifle shots?
Who confronted the Army squad?
Who shot two of the men?
Who detained one?
Who took the man to hospital?
Who described his condition as serious?

(b)   In each case, say whether the evidence is in the **agentive phrase** –
       that is the *by*-phrase – or whether this phrase is deleted and you
       have to infer it from the context.

Commentary

It is possible that we become less aware of people's responsibility for
causing things to happen to others if they are not named, and using a
passive clause is one way of not naming. This does not imply that the
use of the passive always hides essential information, but it may do. For
example, we do not need to know who described the shot man's condition as serious in report (A), but we ought to be told who shot him.
Saying *two of the men were shot* is not as complete a statement as *the
Army squad shot two of the men*.

Exercise 13

(a)   Write down the passive clauses in report (B) and answer these
       questions:

       Who captured the five men?
       Who fired the shots?
       Who replied to plastic bullets with stones?

(b)   Comment on why you can or cannot answer the questions, when
       there are no agentive phrases.

Commentary

There is also in (B) another clear example of the way in which you can avoid naming an actor/agent, and so diminish his or her responsibility for an action, by using the passive voice in a clause and omitting the agentive phrase.

If we try to convert the passive clause *plastic bullets were replied to with stones* into its active form, we cannot supply the subject: *X replied to plastic bullets with stones*.

It must presumably be some of the crowd of mourners, but they are not identified in (B), as they are in (A), as *youths*.

Whether consciously done or not, it is clear that (B) has avoided naming those who *replied* (or *threw*, *bombarded*, *hurled*, *lobbed*, *flung*, *flipped*, *chucked*?) the *stones* (or *paving stones*, *missiles*?) at the soldiers who fired plastic bullets.

This clause also implies quite clearly, without actually saying so, that the Army fired at the mourners first, in the use of the verb *were replied to*. A reply always *follows*.

Therefore it is possible to play down the role of certain actors by using the passive and so not naming them – and this goes unnoticed by most readers. You cannot do this in an active clause, because the actor is also the grammatical subject, and this you cannot omit.

(c)   Grammatical structure; using transformations: To analyse the reports in detail, another useful technique is to 'transform' the varieties of sentence and clause structure of the text into basic 'underlying' structures with the same pattern:

1. *actor/agent* / 2. *action* / 3. *affected* person or thing

as in a simple SPO active clause like *the youths* / *threw* / *stones*, where the surface structure matches the underlying structure.

But in *plastic bullets were replied to with stones*, the surface structure leaves out much of the underlying structure, which contains several statements:

	actor/agent	*action*	*affected*
1.	(soldiers)	(caused):	
2.	**plastic bullets**	(hit)	(people)
3.	(people)	(threw)	**stones**
=		**replied**	

Only the words in bold type appear in the report, so it is clear that the surface structure leaves out a great deal, and that a reader may not notice the real implications and so not ask, 'Who acted first?' and 'Who threw stones?'

Exercise 14

Work through the reports, or take selected parts of them, and reduce the surface forms to their basic patterns of actor / action / affected. (In some cases, there will be no affected or second participant.)

Take each of the four participant groups (the Army, the IRA men, the crowd of mourners, and the youths) in turn, and see how the reports differ in the attribution of responsibility for action.

Then answer these questions:

(a) Is there any significant difference between the two reports in their attribution of action to the Army?

(b) Do the more detailed references to IRA action in (A) affect your understanding of what happened?

(c) Contrast the actions attributed to the mourners in (A) and (B).

With practice you will be able to scan a text and discover its important features without setting it out in such detail, but the methods illustrated help to make sure that you do not miss anything important.

You should now be able to say something positive about selective reporting in newspapers *from the evidence of the texts*, without knowing which papers they are.

Exercise 15

Compare and contrast the following texts, which are extracts from the reports of an incident in the North Yorkshire town of Selby during a national miners' strike. The texts are from two different newspapers.

Use the methods demonstrated in the chapter to examine (i) the connotations of the vocabulary used to name the participants and actions, (ii) the style of presentation. Relate the vocabulary and style to the interpretation of the events likely to be given to the readers of each paper.

(The Selby coalfield was still under development, and contractors were busy in construction work at the mines in the area. Mr Arthur Scargill was President of the National Union of Mineworkers):

Newspaper A (front page with banner headlines)
Headlines, 1st set, front page:

Scargill's storm-troops terrify a town
THE SIEGE OF SELBY
Shoppers' fury over the mobs

2nd set, page 2:

TOWN'S RULE OF TERROR
Flying pickets blockade bridge in dawn swoop

Text:

A town put under mob rule by Arthur Scargill's flying pickets last night demanded: "This must never happen again."

The military style operation in the quiet market town of
Selby involved 4,000 strikers. It left police helpless as   5
five-mile traffic jams rapidly built up.
This is how a town centre shopkeeper – still too afraid
to give his name – last night summed up the siege of
Selby:
"It was nothing more than the rule of the mob. People   10
were terrified. Now many are angry and insisting that
this must not be allowed to happen again."
While the storm-troop battalions were blockading Selby,
Mr Scargill and Coal Board boss Ian MacGregor were meeting
in London in a bid to end the bitter 17-week strike.   15
It was dawn when nearly 600 miners took over the narrow
Selby toll bridge on the A19 which is the only way over
the River Ouse without making a 10-mile detour through
narrow lanes.
With the town now sealed off, more than 500 pickets   20
rampaged through the streets. They terrified shopkeepers
and housewives and overturned a contractor's van.
Said an elderly shopkeeper: "A mob of at least 500 came
down High Street jeering and chanting. It was bedlam."

It was some hours before Selby returned to normal.   25
Pickets later claimed that they had blockaded the town to
stop contractors and materials getting through to the
pits. But police said: "This was just another attempt at
mob rule."

Injured   30

Ten police and four pickets were hurt and there were
four arrests.

Many militant miners fear the new Selby coalfield
because of its rich reserves, high efficiency and low
production costs.   35

They cannot forget that the 4,000 miners who will be
employed at Selby will be able to turn out the same amount
of coal as 20,000 men today.

Newspaper B (page 3, small headlines):
Headlines:

Pickets move on to market town
Selby's arranged marriage strained

Text:

Selby, the market town that is going through an arranged
marriage with the mining community, yesterday experienced
at first hand the effects of the miners' dispute.

Reports of rampaging miners and of the town being under
siege were greatly exaggerated. But the incidents around   5
Selby will probably do the miners little good in a town
that will be of increasing importance to them in the years
to come.

When normality returned yesterday, 10 policemen had been
slightly hurt, one of whom was detained in hospital, three   10
pickets had been taken to hospital but later discharged
and a construction worker had been slightly hurt. Two
police vans and a construction workers' van were
overturned.

The local difficulty began shortly before 6.45 am when   15
about 3,000 miners converged on Selby and avoided police
efforts to stop them.

The miners have been trying to persuade construction workers
not to cross picket lines.

The miners did not stop the construction workers going   20
in and this obviously caused some frustration. Two police
vans were overturned.

Miners later temporarily blockaded the main toll bridge
into Selby. Their peaceful protest drew residents'
grumbles about being delayed for more than two hours.   25

As they dispersed, a group of miners spotted a rented
van being used to take construction workers to the pits.
The van had been held up in the traffic queue.

According to local residents, men surrounded the van and
began banging on the side. They overturned it with the   30
men inside.

9

Variety and style in written English — II. The language of literature

One of the defining features of literature is its special use of language. In many novels and short stories, in drama and especially in verse and poetry, language is itself **foregrounded** or 'made strange'. Its style is different from that of other everyday uses. It is said to deviate from ordinary language. By applying to literary texts the methods of analysis which have been demonstrated on other varieties of English, you can discover interesting facts about the language of literature, and these will help in your evaluation of a literary work.

9.1   The Preacher

The Bible is widely read as literature, and there has been much controversy over the relative merits of new translations of the Bible in comparison with the *Authorised Version* of 1611, which was for centuries the only version of the Bible available to be read and heard in the churches. What makes the Bible literature? What it says, or how it says it?

Here are three versions of a verse from the Old Testament book Ecclesiastes.

Exercise 1

Read the texts, and make your own judgement about their literary qualities before continuing with the commentary.

(1)

    I returned, and saw under the sun, that the race is not to the swift, nor the battle to the strong, neither yet bread to the wise, nor yet riches to men of understanding, nor yet favour to men of skill; but time and chance happeneth to them all.

(2)

Objective consideration of contemporary phenomena compels the conclusion that success or failure in competitive activities exhibits no tendency to be commensurate with innate capacity, but that a considerable element of the unpredictable must invariably be taken into account.

(3)

Using your loaf won't fill your bread-bin, a mystery preacher warned in a pulpit blast yesterday.

And punters will be pipped to know that though the horse they backed is first past the post – they won't pick up their winnings.

HE-MEN have had it, according to the no-holds-barred sermon.

Commentary

Here are three contrasting styles of written English, versions of the same original Hebrew text. Keith Waterhouse concludes his book *Daily Mirror Style* with them.

Do they all say the same thing? You will agree that only the first, from the King James Bible, would be accepted as literary. The second is a **parody** of bureaucratic English, 'officialese', by George Orwell. The third is a **pastiche** written in the style of a tabloid newspaper by Keith Waterhouse himself, but not as an example of good journalism. 'That's not style. But it's what gets into newspapers.' So it is not content that makes a work literary.

The literary version was very much influenced by the language of earlier sixteenth-century translations of the Bible, and so already formal and archaic by the early seventeenth-century. Without a knowledge of ancient Hebrew, it is not possible to know how closely the translation follows the original text, but it would be reasonable to assume that it is as close to the Hebrew as could be achieved.

George Orwell wrote 'Politics and the English Language' in 1946. The parody was intended to illustrate what he called 'staleness of imagery' and 'lack of precision'.

The first contains forty-nine words but only sixty syllables, and all its words are those of everyday life. The second contains thirty-eight words of ninety syllables: eighteen of its words are from Latin roots, and one from Greek. The first sentence contains six vivid images, and only one phrase ('time and chance') that could be called vague. The second contains not a single fresh, arresting phrase, and in spite of its ninety syllables it gives only a shortened version of the meaning contained in the first.

One important difference between the two versions is that (1) uses mostly **concrete** nouns (*sun, race, battle, bread, riches, men*) and simple descriptive adjectives used as nouns (*the swift, the strong, the wise*). The parody has **abstract** nouns, which are less direct in their reference (*considerations, phenomena, conclusion, success, failure,* and so on).

Equally important in (1) is the **parallelism** of the successive clauses and phrases, that is, the grammatical patterns repeat themselves, but with different words:

		the race	is not	to the swift
nor		the battle		to the strong
neither yet		bread		to the wise
nor	yet	riches		to men of understanding
nor	yet	favour		to men of skill

This parallelism of structure is responsible for the strong **rhythm** of the verse when we read it aloud, or hear it read in imagination, as we must if we are to respond to its meaning. You can see that it is poetry. Orwell's parody is not, and the vagueness given to it by the polysyllabled Latinate words in meaning also provides a mushy lack of rhythm.

For these reasons, we can say that (1) is literary, and (2) is not. But what about version (3)?

It seems to have the concreteness of vocabulary of (1) (*loaf, breadbin, preacher, pulpit, blast* etc.), but of course several of these are not used in·their literal sense. Parts of it have some liveliness, a sort of 'falling rhythm',

using your loaf won't fill your bread-bin	/xx/x/x/x
HE-MEN have had it	/xx/x
first past the post	//x/

but this is neither sustained nor very significant.

Keith Waterhouse imitates the practice of most of the tabloid press news reports in writing only one sentence in each paragraph, but its chief feature is the use of colloquial vocabulary and metaphor, which some critics would call *cliché* and reject as bad English without further analysis. On the other hand, you may enjoy this style for its outrageous linking of *using your loaf* ('using your understanding') with *fill your bread-bin* and its double meaning which is both literal, and slang for *belly*.

The second sentence, in its version of 'the race is not to the swift', again uses colloquial words and phrases in a racy alternative. The third has the punch-line, and is consistently informal (*have had it* in the sense of *will fail*, and *no-holds-barred* as a pre-modifier to *sermon*).

This journalistic pastiche is clever and amusing because we respond to it not as journalism, but with the echoes of the Biblical version in our mind, and the absurd contrast makes its own effect. If you do not know the original, then any pastiche will be ineffective. Your reading of any text is strongly affected by what you think it is. The question as to whether it is literature is left for you to debate.

9.2   The Good Samaritan again

Exercise 1

Read the two versions of the parable of the Good Samaritan in chapter 2, and say whether you prefer either version for its literary qualities. Can you then say more precisely what those literary qualities are?

Exercise 2

Then read the following version of the parable, discuss the differences in vocabulary and their effect, and comment on the style of this version in comparison with the first two. Answer these questions:
(a)   Is it a translation?
(b)   Is it the same story?
(c)   Is it literature?

A man was going from his apartment in the project to his friend's house. While he was walking, a couple of muggers jumped him in a dark place. He didn't have very much, so

they took his wallet and clothes and beat on him and
stomped on him – they almost killed him.   5
     Before long a hood came by, but he didn't give a care.
Besides, the cops might ask him questions, so he beat it
out of there. Next came a squeak – never gave the poor
guy a second look. After a while a real cool square comes
along. He sees the character, feels sorry for him. So he   10
puts a couple of Band-aids on, gives him a drink, and a
lift in his car. The square even put him up in a room
some place. Cost him two bucks too!
     So who do you think the best guy was? Well, you got the
message, bud. But you don't have to be a square to show   15
love, and to be sorry for someone, and to help a guy. But
get with it, man – this is what God wants you to do.

9.3   Exercises in style – from the French

The French author, Raymond Queneau, wrote a book called *Exercices
de Style*, which was published in 1947. In it, the same fragment of a
story is told in ninety-nine different versions. It has been translated into
English by Barbara Wright, and was published as *Exercises in Style* in
1958.
     How can you tell the same story ninety-nine times? The translator
has said:

> In the same way as the story *as such* doesn't matter, the
> particular language it is written in doesn't matter as
> such. . . .. Queneau's tour-de-force lies in the fact that the
> simplicity and banality of the material he starts from
> gives birth to so much. . . ..
>   His purpose here, in the *Exercices*, is, I think, a
> profound exploration into the possibilities of language. . . .
> He pushes language around in a multiplicity of directions
> to see what will happen.

To try to tell you the story in advance would only add another
version to Queneau's. His first 'exercise', called *Notation*, is the best

introduction, because it is written like a set of notes for a story – an outline of what happens.

The object of this study is to show how the linguistic features of the writing determine our recognition of the differences between the exercises. You should look at:

(a)   The choice of **vocabulary** – why one word rather than another? What connotations do particular words bring with them? Do some words seem to stand out of their context? Do they form lexical sets?

(b)   The **grammatical** choices – phrase, clause and sentence structures, word and phrase order.

(c)   The kind of **discourse** which the text represents – who is the narrator? From whose point of view is it told? Is it monologue or dialogue?

Other questions will arise in particular exercises. It is easy enough to say in general terms what each one is about, but you must try to answer the question 'How do I know?' in detail.

Here are some of the ninety-nine variations, followed by descriptive commentaries. Read the texts and make descriptive analyses of the vocabulary, grammar and discourse features which make each text distinctive.

Exercise 1: on 'Notation'

(a)   Identify the characters.
(b)   Where does the action take place?
(c)   When does it happen?
(d)   What happens?
(e)   What do you learn about the characters?
(f)   Who is telling the story?

(1) NOTATION

In the S bus, in the rush hour. A chap of about 26,
felt hat with a cord instead of a ribbon, neck too long,
as if someone's been having a tug-of-war with it. People
getting off. The chap in question gets annoyed with one

of the men standing next to him. He accuses him of   5
jostling him every time anyone goes past. A snivelling
tone which is meant to be aggressive. When he sees a
vacant seat he throws himself on to it.

Two hours later, I meet him in the Cour de Rome, in
front of the gare Saint-Lazare. He's with a friend who's   10
saying: 'You ought to get an extra button put on your
overcoat.' He shows him where (at the lapels) and why.

Exercise 2: on 'The Subjective Side'

(a)   Who is telling the story?

(b)   The events are not told in the same order. Why?

(c)   Consider the effect on the narrative, and our impressions of the
       main character (which can only be inferred from the words on
       the page), if some of his words and phrases had been chosen
       differently. Substitute them for what he actually said, and discuss
       what difference of meaning follows:

my clothes	for	my attire
wearing	for	inaugurating
fashionable	for	sprightly
didn't criticise	for	didn't dare attack
complained to	for	roundly told off
a passenger	for	a vulgar type
jostling	for	ill-treating
uncomfortable	for	unspeakably foul
buses	for	omnibi
people	for	hoi polloi
travel on them	for	have to consent to use them

(d)   Do any features of the grammar reinforce your impressions of
       the character?

(2) THE SUBJECTIVE SIDE

I was not displeased with my attire this day. I was
inaugurating a new, rather sprightly hat, and an overcoat
of which I thought most highly. Met X in front of the

gare Saint-Lazare who tried to spoil my pleasure by trying
to prove that this overcoat is cut too low at the lapel   5
and that I ought to have an extra button on it. At least
he didn't dare attack my head-gear.
A bit earlier I had roundly told off a vulgar type who was
purposely ill-treating me every time anyone went by
getting on or off. This happened in one of those   10
unspeakably foul omnibi which fill up with hoi polloi
precisely at those times when I have to consent to use
them.

Exercise 3: on 'Telegraphic'

(a)   Rewrite the text in normal prose.
(b)   What have you had to add to the text to do this?

(3) TELEGRAPHIC

BUS CROWDED STOP YNGMAN LONGNECK PLAITENCIRCLED HAT
APOSTROPHISES UNKNOWN PASSENGER UNAPPARENT REASON STOP
QUERY FINGERS FEET HURT CONTACT HEEL ALLEGED PURPOSELY
STOP YNGMAN ABANDONS DISCUSSION PROVACANT SEAT STOP 1400
HOURS PLACE ROME YNGMAN LISTENS SARTORIAL ADVICE FRIEND
STOP MOVE BUTTON STOP SIGNED ARCTURUS

Commentary: on 'Notation'

The characters:

    (i)   a chap (call him C)
    (ii)   a man (Y)
    (iii)   a friend of C's (X)
    (iv)   the narrator, (I) (N)

The place:

    (i)   in the S bus
    (ii)   in front of the Saint-Lazare railway station in
            the Cour de Rome, Paris

The time:

            Year and day unspecified; 'in the rush hour'
            and 'two hours later'.

The events:

(i)   C accuses Y of jostling him while both are standing in a crowded bus. C takes a vacant seat.

(ii)   X tells C that C needs an extra button on his overcoat.

What else are we told?

(i)   about C:

C is about 26, has a long neck, and wears a hat with a cord instead of a ribbon round it.

We learn something about him from his accusation of Y, his 'snivelling tone' which is meant to be aggressive.

(ii)   about Y, X and N?

Nothing.

This is obviously not a traditional story with a beginning, middle, and end. Nothing happens that would seem to deserve mention. We are led to wonder what Queneau is going to make of it in the 98 following versions. The clue lies in the language, not in the story-line.

Vocabulary

Reference to the characters as *chap*, *man*, *friend* is informal and carries no other connotation.

Notice that C *accuses* Y; the narrator does not say that Y jostles C as a fact, so it may be C's sensitivity that is misplaced. This impression is reinforced by *snivelling*, which implies weakness. C's aggressive intentions are not successfully communicated.

C does not sit down, but throws himself on to a seat. This implies an emotional response – anger or petulance.

Grammar

Two features convey the sense of notes for a story:

(i)   The **minor sentences** in the first paragraph, which lack one or other of the elements usually found in a clause, the subject NP or the predicator VP.

In the S bus, in the rush hour – two **prepositional phrases** (PrepPs), functioning as **adverbials** of place.

A chap of about 26 – an NP.

felt hat . . . ribbon – another NP.

neck too long – the **linking verb** *be* is omitted, and the **possessive pronoun** *his* before the noun.
People getting off – the **auxiliary verb** *be* is omitted.
A snivelling tone . . . aggressive – a complex NP with a qualifying **relative clause**.

(ii)   The use of the **simple present tense**, which is unusual in narrative:

gets annoyed	accuses	goes	is meant
sees	throws	meet	's (= is)
shows			

The only apparent exceptions are:

's been having	(present + perfective + progressive)
's saying	(present + progressive)

which are complex but still present in tense.

Discourse
It is **3rd person** narrative, though the narrator appears to place himself within the events when he says, 'Two hours later, I meet him. . .' But he does not interact with C and X, only observes them.

Commentary: on 'The Subjective Side'

The title is important. This is a subjective point of view, told in the first person by the character C, the 'chap of about 26' in *Notation*, and one of the character sketches.

Discourse
Notice that the order of events is reversed. The event of the day for C is the fact that he is wearing his new hat and overcoat, so this comes first. His meeting with X is related to this, and so the affair on the bus is less important.

The chronological order of events, whether fact (as in newspaper reporting) or fiction (as in novels or short stories), is often rearranged to give prominence to one of them. This is part of what we mean by **plot** in a novel. The amount of space used, as well as order, is also significant.

Our first impression of C in *Notation* is reinforced by his own words.

Vocabulary

If we think of our use of words as making a choice from a number of alternatives when we talk or write, then we can see how style can be viewed as how we say something, which is in addition to our primary choice of what to say, or whether to say it.

Grammar

A number of grammatical features combine to convey the impression of the narrator's voice – perhaps writing a diary? *Met X. . .* suggests this, though it is the only example of the omission of the subject *I*, but the impression is conveyed through the precise formality of the self-confessions that C is making, and the consistency in his character that is built up.

(i)   'I was not displeased with. . .' – a double negative which does convey the positive 'I was pleased with. . .' but with a suggestion of hesitancy or self-deprecation, perhaps.

(ii)   'of which I thought most highly' – partly the lexical choice of 'to think highly of' in relation to an overcoat, but also the formal style of *of which*, avoiding the preposition-at-the-end form of 'which I thought most highly of'. Compare 'which I liked a lot'.

(iii) 'tried to spoil' and 'trying to prove'
       'didn't dare attack'
       'have to consent to use'
       These **catenative** structures of two or more verbs linked by *to* (except with *dare*) also fill in C's character. 'Try to' implies 'didn't succeed'; 'didn't dare' implies the superiority of C in his relationship with X; 'have to' suggests reluctance, and 'consent' condescension.

(iv)   A number of **adverbs** combine also to express C's point of view:
       At least functions as a **sentence adverbial** (or **disjunct**).
       '*roundly* told off' implies C's manner of telling as he imagines it, and '*purposely* ill-treating me' is C's interpretation of Y's behaviour.
       '*unspeakably* foul omnibi', or 'so foul that I can't speak of it' equally gives away C's attitude, and '*precisely* at those times' suggests the (to him) unfortunate concurrence of the rush-hour and his time-table.

The complete subjectivity of the fictional C's account of his day can be readily seen from this analysis of the lexical and grammatical choices which are the means of conveying the discourse.

Commentary: on 'Telegraphic'

Telegrams and cables are charged by the word, so it is cheaper to leave out unessential words, and to compress as much information as possible into single words (making them up if necessary). This can be done by **compounding** and **abbreviating** and by the omission of **function words** which are necessary to construct a grammatical sentence in most other varieties of English. For example, 'YNGMAN LONGNECK' has two words, but 'a young man with a long neck' has seven. (Compare newspaper headlines in chapter 8 and spoken unscripted commentary in chapter 7.)

We can rewrite the telegram to include function words, and to expand compounds and abbreviations, which will also require some reordering of the words and changes of form:

> There is a CROWDED BUS. A YOUNG MAN with a LONG NECK and
> wearing a HAT which is ENCIRCLED by a PLAIT APOSTROPHISES
> a PASSENGER who is UNKNOWN to him for NO APPARENT REASON.
> It is ALLEGED that the passenger made CONTACT with his
> HEEL and it is possible that (= QUERY) the young man's   5
> FINGERS and FEET were HURT. The YOUNG MAN ABANDONS any
> DISCUSSION in order to (= PRO) sit in a VACANT SEAT. At 2
> p.m. (= 1400 HOURS) in the PLACE de ROME the YOUNG MAN
> LISTENS to ADVICE about his overcoat (= SARTORIAL) from a
> FRIEND. He told him he should MOVE a BUTTON.   10

The function words in English (sometimes called **grammatical** words) are the **determiners**, **conjunctions**, **prepositions**, and **pro-words** which contrast with the **lexical words – nouns**, **verbs**, **adjectives** and **adverbs**.

Check this in the rewritten telegram, where the words in capitals are all lexical words.

You will find amusing examples of 'telegraphese' in Evelyn Waugh's novel *Scoop*, about a young man who is sent by mistake to cover a civil war in Africa for the daily newspaper *The Beast*. William Boot is not an experienced journalist, and so the telegrams he sends contain far too many words.

Here is an example of a Boot telegram, with the reply that followed from *The Beast* and Boot's answer to it:

194 VARIETIES OF ENGLISH

THEY HAVE GIVEN US PERMISSION TO GO TO LAKU AND EVERYONE
IS GOING BUT THERE IS NO SUCH PLACE AM I TO GO TOO SORRY
TO BE A BORE BOOT

UNPROCEED LAKUWARD STOP AGENCIES COVERING PATRIOTIC
FRONT STOP REMAIN CONTACTING CUMREDS STOP NEWS EXYOU   5
UNRECEIVED STOP DAILY HARD NEWS ESSENTIALEST STOP
REMEMBER RATES SERVICE CABLES ONE ETSIX PER WORD BEAST

NO NEWS AT PRESENT THANKS WARNING ABOUT CABLING PRICES
BUT IVE PLENTY MONEY LEFT AND ANYWAY WHEN I OFFERED TO
PAY WIRELESS MAN SAID IT WAS ALL RIGHT PAID OTHER END   10
RAINING HARD HOPE ALL WELL ENGLAND WILL CABLE AGAIN IF
ANY NEWS BOOT

Exercise 4

Here is a short selection of openings from the *Exercises in Style* to read.
Identify the foregrounded features of the language. Try to continue
some of them in a similar style, or create your own titles and styles.

(4) ASIDES

The bus arrived bulging with passengers. *Only hope I don't miss
it, oh good, there's still just room for me.* One of them *queer sort of
mug he's got with that enormous neck* was wearing a soft felt hat
with a sort of little plait round it instead of a ribbon *just showing
off that is* and suddenly started *hey what's got into him* to vituperate
his neighbour. . ..

(5) PRECISION

In a bus of the S-line, 10 metres long, 3 wide, 6 high, at 3km.
600 m. from its starting point, loaded with 48 people, at 12.17 p.m.,
a person of the masculine sex aged 27 years 3 months and 8 days,
1m. 72cm. tall and weighing 65kg. . . .

(6) ANAGRAMS

In het S sub in het hurs hour a pach of tabou swinettyx, who had
a glon, hint cken and a tah mmitred with a droc instead of a
borbin . . . .

(7) ONOMATOPOEIA

On the platform, pla pla pla, of a bus, chuff chuff chuff, which was an S (and singing still dost soar, and soaring ever singest), it was about noon, ding dang dong, ding dang dong . . ..

(8) COCKNEY

So A'm stand'n' n' ahtsoider vis frog bus when A sees vis young Froggy bloke, caw bloimey, A finks, 'f'at ain't ve most funniest look'n geezer wot ever A claps eyes on . . ..

(9) FOR ZE FRRENSH

Wurn dayee abaout meeddayee Ahee got eentoo a buss ouich ouoz goeeng een ze deerekssion off ze Porte Champerret. Eet ouoz fool, nearlee . . ..

9.4   Some notes on verse

9.4.1   Rhythm and stress in speech

(i)   Syllable and stress
The rhythm of ordinary English speech derives from the patterns of stress in words and utterances. It is generally agreed that the stressed syllables in speech tend to occur at roughly regular intervals - the technical term is **isochrony** - especially in deliberate speech, for example (-s = unstressed syllable; +s = stressed syllable):

-s +s +s   -s +s   -s-s +s -s -s -s +s
I told John I wasn't aware of all the facts
  1   2   3   4   5

This sentence can be spoken so that the stresses are equally spaced. The number of unstressed syllables between them does not matter - you can have none (between 1 and 2), one (between 2 and 3), two (between 3 and 4), or three (between 4 and 5). More than three tends to be unusual, but theoretically any number is possible.

Exercise 1

Test out this theory of isochronous (equally-spaced) stress by making up some short sentences, or taking some from a book, and reading them aloud. Mark the stressed syllables prominently, and note the number of unstressed syllables between them.

Can you easily speak three or more unstressed syllables between the stresses?

(ii)   The foot
The stretch of sound from one stress up to, but not including, the next stress, has been called a **foot**:

> / ∧ I / **told** / **John** I/**wasn't** aw/**are** of all the / **facts**
>   1   2   3   4   5   6

This sentence has six feet. Because a foot begins with a stress, we have to think of some stresses as having no sound and refer to a **silent stress** in the first foot of the sentence, marked with ∧.

Some linguists, however, do not accept the need for the concept of a foot in the spoken language, nor in the **scansion** of verse. But it is briefly mentioned because you may come across the term or want to use it.

9.4.2   Metre
The basis of the patterns of verse is a 'heightening' of this tendency towards a regular succession of stressed syllables, or stress-timed rhythm, which is called **metre**. The regularity of stress is **foregrounded**. Verse is usually metrical in its structure. (If its rhythm is not regular, it is called free verse.)

It is useful to distinguish between the stress-patterns of ordinary speech and poetic metre by referring to **beats** (B) and **off-beats** (o) in the metre of verse, and **stressed** (+s) and **unstressed** (-s) syllables in speech. English metrical verse therefore consists of alternate beats and off-beats.

So the rhythm of verse is a kind of **counterpoint** between the regular pattern of beats and off-beats (metre) underlying the natural pattern of stressed and unstressed syllables of the spoken language. The clash between the two often has an important effect on the rhythm and meaning. Sometimes unstressed syllables have to be **promoted** to metrical beats, or stressed syllables **demoted** to off-beats. A metrical off-beat can consist of one, two or three unstressed syllables, called **single off-beats** (o), **double off-beats** (ŏ) and **triple off-beats** (ŏ̤), just as there are a variable number of unstressed syllables between the stresses in ordinary speech.

The pleasure that children get from traditional nursery rhymes is very largely derived from the rhythms, together with rhyme and the other patterns of sound which will be discussed later.

Look for example at 'Three Blind Mice':

(x = unstressed syllable; ^ = silent stress; stressed syllables are in **bold** type)

	Three	x	x	**blind**	x	x	**mice**	x	x	^	x		x
	See	x	x	**how**	x	they	**run**	x	x	^	x		
They	**all**	x	ran	**af**	-ter	the	**far**	x	-mer's	**wife**	x		
Who	**cut**	off	their	**tails**	with	a	**car**	x	-ving	**knife**	x		
Did	**ev**	-er	you	**see**	such	a	**thing**	in	your	**life**	x		
As	**three**	x	x	**blind**	x	x	**mice**	x	x	^	x		x
metre:	B		ŏ	B		ŏ	B		ŏ	B		ŏ	

There are four beats to a line. The metre is **triple**, with a double off-beat (= two unstressed syllables) between each beat, but the first two lines have only three syllables each, so you have to stretch them to cover the rhythmic space of nine syllables altogether – three stressed and six unstressed, and then pause for the silent beat and double off-beat. Silent beats and off-beats are as important as the spoken ones in metrical verse.

Exercise 2

Many nursery rhymes have triple rhythms. Match the syllable and stress patterns of the following rhymes to their underlying metre of beats and off-beats.

> There was an old woman who lived in a shoe,
> She had so many children she didn't know what to do;
> She gave them some broth without any bread;
> She whipped them all soundly and put them to bed.

(The only problem is *didn't know what to do*.)

> Little Bo-peep has lost her sheep,
> And can't tell where to find them;
> Leave them alone and they'll come home,
> Bringing their tails behind them

Other rhymes have **duple rhythm**, that is, there is a single off-beat between each beat. Here is one that is completely regular:

> I **do** not **love** thee **Doc**tor **Fell**,
> o B   o   B   o   B   o   B
> The **reason** **why** I **cannot** **tell**,
> o   B   o   B o B   o   B
> But **this** I **know**, I **know** full **well**,
> o   B o B   o B   o   B
> I **do** not **love** thee **Doc**tor **Fell**.
> o B   o   B   o   B   o   B

Because the rhythm of the lines in 'Doctor Fell' moves regularly from an off-beat to a beat, it is called a **rising** rhythm. Conversely, a rhythm regularly beginning with a beat and moving to the off-beat is called a **falling** rhythm, as in

> **Doc**tor **Bell** fell **down** the **well**
> B   o   B   o   B   o   B
> And broke his **collar** **bone**.
> o   B   o B o B [o B o]
> **Doc**tors **should** at**tend** the **sick**
> B   o   B   o   B   o   B
> And **leave** the **well** a**lone**.
> o   B   o   B o B [o B o]

It is important to establish the metre of a poem, because part of its meaning, and a great deal of the pleasure it gives, lie in the rhythm.

Exercise 3

Read these two sentences aloud, and say where the main stresses fall.
(a)   Here was the former door where the dead feet walked in.
(b)   She sat here in her chair, smiling into the fire.

Commentary

There is no one right way of reading them, but if the sentences are read in the rhythm of ordinary speech, do you agree that in (a) the main stresses will fall on *door*, *feet* and *walked*, with secondary stress on *former* and *dead*, and that in (b) the main stresses are on *sat*, *chair*, *smiling* and *fire*?

Exercise 4

Now read the same sentences in the context of Thomas Hardy's poem 'The Self-Unseeing'. Establish the metrical pattern from the third stanza, which is quite regular, and than apply the same pattern to the first two stanzas.

Does it make you read the two sentences already discussed in a different way? What contribution to the meaning of the poem does this revised reading make?

> Here is the ancient floor,
> Footworn and hollow and thin,
> Here was the former door
> Where the dead feet walked in.
>
> She sat here in her chair,   5
> Smiling into the fire;
> He who played stood there,
> Bowing it higher and higher.
>
> Childlike I danced in a dream;
> Blessings emblazoned that day;   10
> Everything glowed with a gleam;
> Yet we were looking away!

Commentary

The underlying metre is a four-line stanza, each line having three beats plus a silent stress, or unrealised beat, at the end of each line, in falling rhythm. In stanza 3 the rhythm is always triple (/xx, B ŏ), but it varies between duple and triple in the other two.
Read in this metre, the two sentences scan like this:

Here was the **for**mer **door**
B   ŏ   B   o   B   [o B o]
Where the dead **feet** walked **in**.
B   ŏ   B   o   B   [o B o]

which is possibly acceptable. But it is very common in English verse to
have two beats together, preceded by an off-beat, and with an implied
or silent off-beat (ô) between them:

Where the **dead feet** walked in
ŏ   B ô B   o   B   [o B o]

Similarly, you can read the regular scansion,

She sat **here** in her **chair**
B   o   B   ŏ   B   [o B o]

or   **She** **sat here** in her **chair**
o   B ô B   ŏ   B   [o B o]

Is it more important to stress *she*, in reference to the dead woman,
or to the fact that she sat? Here perhaps the underlying metre supplies
the answer.

There is much more to say about the rhythm of English verse, but
this brief outline should help to draw your attention to the importance
of establishing a reading which agrees with the poet's setting out of his
verse.

9.4.3   The line in verse

The line is part of the grammar of verse. It establishes a way of hearing
the rhythm which has no equivalent in prose, and affects the meaning
also by focusing attention on particular words.

Exercise 5

Read the following short prose texts aloud, and establish a natural
speech rhythm which seems best to fit them.

(a)   April is the cruellest month, breeding lilacs out of the dead land, mixing memory and desire, stirring dull roots with spring rain. Winter kept us warm, covering earth in forgetful snow, feeding a little life with dry tubers.

(b)   As the cat climbed over the top of the jamcloset, first the right forefoot, carefully, then the hind stepped down into the pit of the empty flowerpot.

(c)   A snake came to my water-trough on a hot, hot day, and I in pyjamas for the heat, to drink there. In the deep, strange-scented shade of the great dark carob-tree I came down the steps with my pitcher and must wait, must stand and wait, for there he was at the trough before me.

(d)   Cut grass lies frail: brief is the breath mown stalks exhale. Long, long the death it dies in the white hours of young-leafed June with chestnut flowers, with hedges snowlike strewn, white lilac bowed, lost lanes of Queen Anne's lace, and that high-builded cloud moving at summer's pace.

Exercise 6

(a)   All four texts of exercise 5 are in fact poems, or parts of poems, printed as prose. Write them out as verse, using other linguistic features associated with verse, as well as rhythm and metre, to establish the lines. (b) and (d) also have a stanza pattern.

(b)   Discuss any difficulties you have in establishing a pattern of lines and stanzas in each poem.

Commentary

(a)   Is the opening of T.S.Eliot's 'The Waste Land':

> April is the cruellest month, breeding
> Lilacs out of the dead land, mixing
> Memory and desire, stirring
> Dull roots with spring rain.
> Winter kept us warm, covering   5
> Earth in forgetful snow, feeding
> A little life with dried tubers.

The line as a rhythmic unit now places strong stress on each of the participles *breeding*, *mixing*, *stirring*, *covering*, and *feeding*, because coming at the end of their lines, there is tension between the natural instinct, based on the sentence grammar (predicator followed by object), to run straight on, and the 'line grammar', which makes us pause on the words, and focus upon them. Notice also that the first two lines have five beats, and the next five lines have four beats. It is a careful balance of rhythm and syntax which underlies the evocation of the 'Waste Land' people's mood.

(b)   Is a poem by the American William Carlos Williams, and called simply 'Poem':

> As the cat
> climbed over
> the top of
>
> the jamcloset
> first the right   5
> forefoot
>
> carefully
> then the hind
> stepped down
>
> into the pit of   10
> the empty
> flowerpot

The punctuation lies wholly in the visual display of four three line stanzas. Williams breaks syntactic units to create his brief lines. In *into the pit of* / *the empty* / *flowerpot* the break comes between the preposition and noun phrase of a prepositional phrase, and between the adjective and noun of a noun phrase. There is no rhyme, assonance or other traditional poetic devices of language. He does not observe the convention of beginning each line with a capital letter. It is a moment of precise observation captured and then communicated through the matching precision required to read the poem line by line. We *read* it as a poem.

(c) Is the opening of D.H.Lawrence's 'Snake'. It is **free verse** and close to normal speech in its rhythm. It is doubtful if you can recreate Lawrence's own presentation, because it is non-metrical, like the Williams poem:

A snake came to my water-trough
On a hot, hot day, and I in pyjamas for the heat,
To drink there.

In the deep, strange-scented shade of the great dark carob-tree
I came down the steps with my pitcher   5
And must wait, must stand and wait, for there he was at the
trough before me.

Lawrence's lines vary in length, and create an impression of the
spoken voice, although there are other features which would seem less
usual in prose – *a hot, hot day*, *I in pyjamas*, and the repetition of
must stand and wait. The line between poetry and prose is not clear. We
speak of 'poetic prose' when prose takes on rhythm or other figures and
patterns which are more often associated with poetry.

   (d)   Is a Philip Larkin poem, 'Cut Grass', and the rhyme should
have made it easy to find the metrical pattern of four four-line stanzas.
The rhythm is subtly varied, and has an underlying falling triple rhythm
with two beats in the line:

               Cut grass lies frail:
               Brief is the breath
               Mown stalks exhale.
               Long, long the death

               It dies in the white hours   5
               Of young-leafed June
               With chestnut flowers,
               With hedges snowlike strewn,

               White lilac bowed,
               Lost lanes of Queen Anne's lace,   10
               And that high-builded cloud
               Moving at summer's pace.

   Notice that the stanzas are not complete grammatical units, so that
there is a tension between metrical pattern and syntactic meaning.

9.4.4   Grammatical deviance in verse

The phrase **poetic licence** refers to the expectation that poets and
writers take liberties with language and meaning in creating literature.

This is also called **deviance**, and examples can be found in poets' use of language at all its levels – sound, vocabulary, grammar, and meaning. The nineteenth-century poet Gerard Manley Hopkins said that poetic language should be 'the current language **heightened**,' and the word *foregrounding* has already been used to refer to this feature of the literary use of language.

One example of grammatical deviance in verse which is very common is a rearrangement of the unmarked order of the elements in a clause (SPOA, subject, followed by predicator, followed by object, followed by adverbial). Similarly in a sentence the unmarked order is main clause followed by subordinate clause.

Exercise 6

A.E. Housman's poem 'On Wenlock Edge' is printed below with the syntax rearranged to show clause and sentence structure in unmarked order. One or two other small alterations have been made to make the grammar more 'normal'.

(a)   Write out the poem as you think Housman wrote it. The rhyme pattern in each stanza is *abab*. Each line has four beats, in a rising duple rhythm.

(b)   All the words of the original poem are in the rewritten version. What has happened to Housman's poem in the process of rewriting?

> The wood's in trouble on Wenlock Edge;
>   The Wrekin heaves his forest fleece;
> The gale plies the saplings double,
>   And the leaves snow thick on Severn.
>
> It would blow like this through holt and hanger   5
>   When the city Uricon stood:
> It is the old wind in the old anger,
>   But then it threshed another wood.
>
> The Roman would stare at yonder heaving hill
>   Then, (it was before my time):   10
> The blood that warms an English yeoman,
>   And the thoughts that hurt him, they were there.
>
> The gale of life blew high through him
>   There, like the wind through woods in riot;

The tree of man was never quiet: 15
   It was the Roman then, now it is I.

The gale plies the saplings double,
   It blows so hard, it will be gone soon:
The Roman and his trouble are
   Ashes under Uricon today.   20

9.4.5 Patterns of rhythm and sound in verse

Pleasure in the rhythms of verse is inseparable from pleasure in the sounds - the patterning of vowels and consonants - and the fusion of sound, rhythm, and meaning is a mark of poetry. Gerard Manley Hopkins' poetry is an outstanding example of this fusion. His sonnet 'God's Grandeur' is typical in its complexity of patterning. Here are the first four lines:

    The world is charged with the grandeur of God.
      It will flame out, like shining from shook foil;
      It gathers to a greatness, like the ooze of oil
    Crushed. Why do men then now not reck his rod?

Exercise 7

The traditional metre of a line of a sonnet is a rising duple rhythm of five beats to a line. Apply this to Hopkins' lines to establish the rhythmic pattern first of all, and therefore the five words given meaningful prominence in each line. You will find that lines 1 and 4 especially will read differently from normal speech.

Commentary

The rhythmic pattern of the lines can be analysed as:

    The **world** is **charged with** the **grand**eur of **God**.
   o   B o   B ŏB o B   ŏ B
    It will **flame out**, like shining from **shook foil**;
   ŏ   B ŏB o B   ŏ   B ŏB

It gathers to a greatness, like the ooze of oil
  o B   ŏ B o B o B o B
Crushed. Why do men then now not reck his rod?
 ô   B   ŏ B o B o B o B

Notice how the underlying 5-beat rhythm makes you stress *with* in line 1, *out* in line 2, and *like* in line 3, which you would not do if the lines were read as prose, or as 4-beat lines. It affects the meaning by focusing attention on these words.

The repetition of the same or similar sounds in words leads to a 'partial correspondence' between them, or **parallelism**. Here are some examples from other Hopkins poems:

rhyme	cow – plough
	things – wings
alliteration	glory – God (initial consonants)
	asunder – starlight
	in – ecstasy (initial vowels)
assonance	caught – morning (medial vowels)
pararhyme	fickle – freckle (initial and
	final consonants)
consonance	rose – moles (final consonants)

These patterns usually apply to the stressed syllables of a line, or adjacent lines, and the sounds must be fairly close together to be effective. Notice that there can be alliteration and consonance between medial consonants of words, that is, consonants beginning or ending syllables within a word, e.g. mystery – stressed.

Exercise 8

What patterns of sound are there in the four lines of 'God's Grandeur' ?

Commentary

The sound pattern is complex, and includes:

rhyme	God – rod

	foil – oil
	men – then
alliteration	world – with
	grandeur – God
	flame – foil
	shining from – shock foil
	gathers – greatness
	ooze – oil
	reck – rod
assonance	men – reck
	shining – like
consonance	world – charged – God

If you think that this is too ingenious, remember that you must hear the counterpoint of sounds, and not just look for them on the page. Hopkins deliberately created these patterns, and said:

> Poetry is speech framed for the contemplation of the mind by the way of hearing, or speech framed to be heard *for its own sake* and interest over and above its interest of meaning.

Exercise 9

Look for the patterns of rhythm and sound in this extract from Hopkins' poem 'The Wreck of the Deutschland' :

Oh,
We lash with the best or worst
Word last! How a lush-kept plush-capped sloe
Will, mouthed to flesh-burst,
Gush! – flush the man, the being with it, sour or sweet
Brim, in a flash, full!

9.5   Dialect in literature

Writers use non-standard language in novels and short stories to tell us that their characters speak in a regional or social dialect. If we read of a woman saying, 'I wonder if you would mind shutting the window?', we know that she is being polite, and assume that she is 'speaking without an accent'. That is, we presume she is using RP.

So it is assumed that a character in a novel or story or play is speaking RP unless we are told otherwise, and writers use certain conventions to show distinctive pronunciation, which itself is often a marker of social class, and includes a few forms of RP, like the aristocratic 'huntin', shootin' and fishin' '.

Because our accent gives away our social class or regional dialect, or both, then the same judgement is made on fictitious characters. This can be done in written English only by changing the usual spelling of words. You will seldom find that writers show dialect consistently or in great detail, and certain conventions have developed for representing dialect and accent in this way.

Exercise 1

Here is an extract from Charles Dickens' *Pickwick Papers*. The non-standard words are printed in bold type. Describe them in relation to Standard English and RP, and suggest what the purpose of this presentation of Sam Weller's speech is.

> Mr Weller proceeded to unpack the basket with the utmost
> dispatch.
>   '**Weal** pie,' said Mr Weller, soliloquising, as he
> arranged the eatables on the grass. '**Wery** good thing is
> **weal** pie, when you know the lady **as** made it, and **is** quite   5
> sure that it **an't** kittens; and **arter** all though, where's
> the odds, when they're so like **weal** that the **wery** piemen
> themselves don't know the difference? I lodged in the
> same house **vith** a pieman once, sir, and a **wery** nice man he
> was – make pies out **o'** anything, he could. "Mr Weller,"   10
> says he, **a squeezing** my hand **wery** hard, and **vispering** in
> my ear – "don't mention **this here agin** – but it's the
> **seasonin'** as does it. They're all made **o'** them noble
> animals," says he, **a pointin'** to a **wery** nice little tabby
> kitten, "and I **seasons** 'em for beefsteak, **weal** or kidney,   15
> **'cordin'** to the demand, just as the market changes, and
> appetites **wary**!"'

Commentary

Sam Weller is one of Dickens' most popular characters, and speaks the London Cockney dialect of the early nineteenth-century. We can list the dialectal features in groups:

1. Its most obvious characteristic is the reversal of /v/ and /w/ when they are word-initial, that is, when the consonants are the first sounds in words.

2. *An't* indicates the pronunciation which has been discussed in the *Acceptability Test* in chapter 1.

3. 'the lady as made it', 'the seasonin' as does it – non-standard relative pronoun *as*, for *who*, *which* or *that*.

4. 'is quite sure', with *you* as subject, and 'I seasons 'em' – non-standard agreement of verb with subject.

5. 'arter all' – spelling shows pronunciation.

6. 'out o' anything' shows pronunciation, and many speakers when talking quickly and informally would reduce *of* in this way. But it *looks* non-standard, and writers often use this way of indicating a speaker from the lower social classes.

    It is sometimes referred to as **eye-dialect**. Compare the spelling of 'What did he say?' and 'Wot did 'e say?' Both sound the same in speech. Which one is the uneducated speaker?

7. 'a squeezing', 'a pointin'' – a form of the **present participle** which still retains a prefix common in Middle English.

8. 'this here agin' – 'this here' is still a common spoken phrase in spoken English; 'agin' is a marked Cockney pronunciation.

9. 'seasonin'', 'pointin'', ''cordin'' – the common pronunciation of word-final /ɪŋ/, spelt ⟨-ing⟩, as /ɪn/. The apostrophe doesn't in fact mark a lost ⟨g⟩, because this isn't pronounced in most English dialects today (except for example in parts of Lancashire). Notice that Dickens doesn't systematically show this in Sam's speech.

The effect of this representation of Sam Weller's speech is to help us to tune in to his Cockney wit and humour. It becomes a part of Sam's character.

Exercise 2

Apply the same principles of identification and description to the non-standard spellings in the following extracts. What do they suggest about the characters? The non-standard items are printed in bold type in the first extract, but not in the other.

(1)
    'And you are a miner!' she exclaimed in surprise.

    'Yes. I went down when I was ten.'

    'When you were ten! And wasn't it very hard?' she asked.

    'You soon get used to it. You live like **th'** mice, **an'**   5
you pop out at night to see what's going on.'

    'It makes me feel blind,' she frowned.

    'Like a **mouldiwarp!**' he laughed. '**Yi, an'** there's some
chaps **as does** go round like **mouldiwarps.**' He thrust his
face forward in the blind, snout-like way of a mole,   10
seeming to sniff and peer for direction. 'They **dun**
though!' he protested naively. '**Tha niver seed** such a way
they get in. But **tha mun** let me **ta'e thee** down some time,
an' tha can see for **thysen.**'

    She looked at him, startled.   15

    'Shouldn't **ter** like it?' he asked tenderly. ''**Appen** not,
it '**ud** dirty **thee.**'

                            (D. H. Lawrence, *Sons and Lovers*)

(2)
Urmilla hardly slept for thinking of what she was going to
do. She got up determined and went to Rita.

    'Girl, I in big trouble. Big, big trouble. If you know
what Tiger go and do! He go and invite two Americans he
does work with to come for Indian food tonight!'   5

    'Is wat happen to him at all? He crack? He is ah dam
fool in truth. He bringing wite people to eat in dat hut?
Tiger must be really going out of he head, yes. Gul, yuh
making joke!'

    'Man, Rita, I tell you is true! My head hot! I don't   10
know what to to. Rita, you go have to help me, girl.'

    'But sure, man. Wat yuh want me to do?'

    'You have to lend me plenty thing. I want glass.
Plate. Cup. Spoon, Knife. Fork. Tablecloth –'

'Take ease, keep cool! Between de two ah we we go fix   15
up everything good. Don't look so frighten. Why de hell
yuh fraid Tiger so? Allyuh Indian people have some funny
ways, *oui*. Well, look. You don't worry bout nutting. Ah
go help you to do everyting.'

(Samuel Selvon, *A Brighter Sun*)

Booklist

Glossary: Teachers and lecturers are recommended to refer to David Crystal's *A First Dictionary of Linguistic and Phonetics* (Deutsch, 1980), or to the index of any descriptive grammar or introductory study of language, for definitions of linguistic terminology used in this book.

The following list contains a selection of books which are mainly intended for reference by teachers and lecturers, though some are written for non-specialists and may be suitable for classroom use. Books with accompanying cassette tapes of spoken data are marked with an asterisk *.

1 Variety, change, and the idea of correct English

D. Crystal, *Who Cares about English Usage?* (Harmondsworth: Penguin, 1984)

W.H. Mittins *et al*, *Attitudes to English Usage* (Oxford University Press, 1970)

W.R. O'Donnell and L. Todd, *Variety in Contemporary English* (London: Allen & Unwin, 1980)

Randolph Quirk, *The Use of English*, 2nd edn. (London: Longman, 1968)

E. Ryan and H. Giles, *Attitudes towards Language Variation* (London: Edward Arnold, 1982)

P. Trudgill, *Accent, Dialect and the School* (London: Edward Arnold, 1975)

P. Trudgill, *Sociolinguistics: an introduction* (Harmondsworth: Penguin, 1974)

2 Dialects and Standard English – the past

C. Barber, *Early Modern English* (London: André Deutsch, 1976)

A.C. Baugh and T. Cable, *A History of the English Language* (London: Routledge & Kegan Paul, 1978)

G.L. Brook, *A History of the English Language* (London: André Deutsch, 1963)

D. Leith, *A Social History of English* (London: Routledge & Kegan Paul, 1983)

S. Potter, *Our Language* (Harmondsworth: Penguin, 1950)

3 Dialects and Standard English – the present

G.L. Brook, *English Dialects* (London: André Deutsch, 1963)

A. Hughes and P. Trudgill, **English Accents & Dialects* (London: Edward Arnold, 1979)

D. Sutcliffe, *British Black English* (Oxford: Basil Blackwell, 1982)

L. Todd, *Modern Englishes: Pidgins and Creoles* (Oxford: Basil Blackwell, 1984)

L. Todd, *'Some Day Been Dey': West African Pidgin Folk Tales* (London: Routledge & Kegan Paul, 1979)

P. Trudgill and J. Hannah, **International English* (London: Edward Arnold, 1982)

M. Wakelin, *Discovering English Dialects*, 2nd edn. (Princes Risborough: Shire Publications, 1979)

4 Regional accents and Received Pronunciation

G. Brown, *Listening to Spoken English* (London: Longman, 1977)

A.C. Gimson, *An Introduction to the Pronunciation of English*, 3rd edn. (London: Edward Arnold, 1980) (standard reference text)

J.C. Wells, **Accents of English*: 1, *Introduction;* 2. *The British Isles*; 3. *Beyond the British Isles* (Cambridge University Press, 1982)

5 Spoken English and written English

D. Crystal and D. Davy, *Advanced Conversational English* (London: Longman, 1975)

M. Stubbs, *Language and Literacy* (London: Routledge & Kegan Paul, 1980)

J. P. French, *Spoken English* (London: Macmillan, 1987)

R. Wardhaugh, *How Conversation Works* (Blackwell, 1987)

6 Learning to talk

J. and P. de Villiers, *Early Language* (London: Fontana, 1979)

M. Fletcher and P. Garman, *Language Acquisition: studies in first language development* (Cambridge University Press, 1979)

7 Variety and style in spoken English

D. Crystal and D. Davy, *Investigating English Style* (London: Longman, 1969)

M. Stubbs, *Discourse Analysis* (Oxford: Basil Blackwell, 1983)

8 Reporting the news

D. Bolinger, *Language the Loaded Weapon: the use and abuse of language today* (London: Longman, 1980)

R. Fowler *et al.*, *Language and Control* (London: Routledge & Kegan Paul, 1979)

G. Kress and R. Hodge, *Language as Ideology* (London: Routledge & Kegan Paul, 1979)

G. Lakoff and M. Johnson, *Metaphors we live by* (University of Chicago Press, 1980)

(In chapter 8, the analysis of newspaper reporting derives from R. Fowler *et al.*, *Language and Control*, chapters 6 - 8.)

9   The language of literature

D. Attridge, *The Rhythms of English Poetry* (London: Longman, 1983)

N.F. Blake, *Non-standard Language in English Literature* (London: André Deutsch, 1981)

N.F. Blake, *Shakespeare's Language: an Introduction* (London: Macmillan, 1983)

R. Carter (ed.), *Language and Literature* (London: Allen & Unwin, 1982)

R. Chapman, *The Language of English Literature* (London: Edward Arnold, 1982)

G. Leech, *A Linguistic Guide to English Poetry* (London: Longman, 1969)

G. Leech and A. Short, *Style in Fiction* (London: Longman, 1981)

H. Widdowson, *Stylistics and the Teaching of Literature* (London: Longman, 1975)

(In chapter 9, section 9.5, the distinction between spoken stress and metrical beat comes from D. Attridge, *The Rhythms of English Poetry*.)

General language study and linguistics

Jean Aitchison, *Language Change: Progress or Decay?* (London: Fontana, 1981)

Anthony Burgess, *Language Made Plain* (London: Fontana, 1975)

R. Carter (ed.), *Linguistics and the Teacher* (London: Routledge & Kegan Paul, 1982)

D. Crystal, *What is Linguistics?* (London: Edward Arnold, 1968)

V. Fromkin and R. Rodman, *An Introduction to Language, 3rd edn.* (New York: Holt, Rinehart & Winston, 1983)

R. Hudson, *Invitation to Linguistics* (Oxford: Robertson, 1984)

English grammar

D. Freeborn, *A Course Book in English Grammar* (London: Macmillan, 1987)

G. Leech, M. Deuchar and R. Hoogenraad, *English Grammar for Today* (London: Macmillan, 1982)

R. Quirk *et al.*, *A Comprehensive Grammar of the English Language* (London: Longman 1985) (standard reference grammar)

G. Leech and J. Svartvik, *A Communicative Grammar of English* (London: Longman, 1975)

R. Quirk and S. Greenbaum, *University Grammar of English* (London: Longman, 1973) (both the last two entries derived from the preceding grammar)

Index

217